Family Bible Study

THE
Herschel
HOBBS
COMMENTARY®

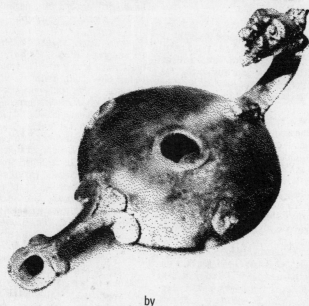

by
Robert J. Dean

SPRING 2002
Volume 2, Number 3

ROSS H. McLAREN
Biblical Studies Specialist

Carolyn Gregory
Production Specialist

Stephen Smith
Graphic Designer

Frankie Churchwell
Technical Specialist

Send questions/comments to
  Ross H. McLaren, editor
  One LifeWay Plaza
  Nashville, TN 37234-0175
  Email: HHobbsComm@lifeway.com

Management Personnel

Louis B. Hanks, *Acting Director*
Adult Sunday School Ministry Department
Louis B. Hanks, *Associate Director*
Sunday School Group
BILL L. TAYLOR, *Director*
Sunday School Group

ACKNOWLEDGMENTS.–We believe the Bible has God for its author; salvation for its end; and truth, without any mixture of error, for its matter and that all Scripture is totally true and trustworthy. The 2000 statement of *The Baptist Faith and Message* is our doctrinal guideline.

Unless otherwise indicated, all Scripture quotations are from the *King James Version.* This translation is available in a Holman Bible and can be ordered through LifeWay Christian Stores. Scripture quotations identified as CEV are from the *Contemporary English Version.* Copyright © American Bible Society 1991, 1992. Used by permission. Quotations marked GNB or TEV are from the *Good News Bible,* the Bible in Today's Modern English Version. Old Testament: Copyright © American Bible Society 1976; New Testament: Copyright © American Bible Society 1966, 1971, 1976. Used by permission. Quotations marked HCSB have been taken from the *Holman Christian Standard Bible,* © Copyright 2000 by Broadman & Holman Publishers. Used by permission. This translation is available in a Holman Bible and can be ordered through LifeWay Christian Stores. Passages marked NASB are from the *New American Standard Bible: 1995 Update.* © The Lockman Foundation, 1960, 1962, 1963, 1968, 1971, 1972, 1973, 1975, 1977, 1995. Used by permission. This translation is available in a Holman Bible and can be ordered through LifeWay Christian Stores. Quotations marked NEB are from *The New English Bible.* Copyright © The Delegates of the Oxford University Press and the Syndics of the Cambridge University Press, 1961, 1970. Reprinted by permission. Quotations marked NIV are from the *Holy Bible, New International Version,* copyright © 1973, 1978, 1984 by International Bible Society (NIVmg. = NIV margin). This translation is available in a Holman Bible and can be ordered through Lifeway Christian Stores. Excerpts marked NJB are from *The New Jerusalem Bible,* copyright © 1985 by Darton, Longman and Todd, Ltd., and Doubleday and Company, Inc. Used by permission of the publisher. Quotations marked NKJV are from the *New King James Version.* Copyright © 1979, 1980, 1982. Thomas Nelson, Inc., Publishers. Reprinted with permission. This translation is available in a Holman Bible and can be ordered through Lifeway Christian Stores. Quotations marked NRSV are from the *New Revised Standard Version of the Bible,* copyright © 1989 by the Division of Christian Education of the National Council of the Churches of Christ in the United States of America. Used by permission. All rights reserved. Quotations marked REB are from *The Revised English Bible.* Copyright © Oxford University Press and Cambridge University Press, 1989. Reprinted by permission.

Family Bible Study: The Herschel Hobbs Commentary® (ISSN 0191-4219), is published quarterly for adult teachers and members using the Family Bible Study series by LifeWay Christian Resources of the Southern Baptist Convention, One LifeWay Plaza, Nashville, Tennessee 37234, Gene Mims, President, LifeWay Church Resources, a division of LifeWay Christian Resources; James T. Draper, Jr., President, Ted Warren, Executive Vice-President, LifeWay Christian Resources; Bill L. Taylor, Director, Sunday School Group. © Copyright 2001 LifeWay Christian Resources of the Southern Baptist Convention. All rights reserved. Single subscription to individual address, $20.95 per year. If you need help with an order, WRITE LifeWay Church Resources Customer Service, One LifeWay Plaza, Nashville, Tennessee 37234-0113; For subscriptions, FAX (615) 251-5818 or EMAIL subscribe@lifeway.com. For bulk shipments mailed quarterly to one address, FAX (615) 251-5933 or EMAIL CustomerService@lifeway.com. Order ONLINE at www.lifeway.com. Mail address changes to: *The Herschel Hobbs Commentary, Family Bible Study,* One LifeWay Plaza, Nashville, TN 37234-0113.

Dedicated to the memory of

Bill Burgess,

who cared deeply

for his church, his family, and his friends.

Contents

Study Theme

EIGHT DAYS THAT CHANGED THE WORLD   6

Study Theme

Amos: Prophet to the Nations   55

Contents

Study Theme

Being God's Agent in Crisis Times   96

Study Theme

Eight Days That Changed the World

Jesus made His royal entry into Jerusalem on a Sunday, which we call Palm Sunday. He was raised from the dead on the following Sunday. About one-third of the Gospels' content tells of these events and those in between. These were the "Eight Days That Changed the World." According to A. T. Robertson, on Monday Jesus cleansed the temple. On Tuesday He taught in the temple about the end times. On Thursday Jesus had His disciples prepare for the last supper. He ate with them and instituted the Lord's Supper on that evening, which by Jewish reckoning was on Friday (their days began at sunset). Also on that night Jesus taught the disciples the truths found in John 14–16 and prayed the prayer of John 17. His prayer in Gethsemane, His arrest, and His trials took place late that night. On Friday He was crucified and buried. His body lay in the tomb on Saturday. On the first day of the week He appeared alive to His followers.[1]

This five-session study theme will devote four sessions to Jesus' teachings in John 14–16 and to Jesus' prayer in John 17. These teachings often are called teachings from the upper room or Jesus' farewell discourse. This material is found only in John's Gospel. Since Jesus gave these teachings and prayed this prayer on His last night before His crucifixion, they represent the highest revelation before the cross and resurrection. These chapters contain some of the most treasured words of Jesus. The final lesson on Easter is based on 1 Corinthians 15.

This study is designed to help you:
- grow in your knowledge of, and experience with, God (Mar. 3)
- be productive for Christ (Mar. 10)
- allow the Holy Spirit to continue Christ's work through you (Mar. 17)
- work toward unity among God's people (Mar. 24)
- live each day in anticipation of the resurrection (Mar. 31)

[1]A. T. Robertson, *A Harmony of the Gospels* [New York: Harper & Brothers Publishers, 1932], 152-246.

Week of March 3

KNOWING GOD

Bible Passage: John 14:1-14
Key Verses: John 14:6-7

❖ *Significance of the Lesson*

• The *Theme* of this lesson is Jesus is the only way to know God.
• The *Life Question* this lesson seeks to address is, How can I know God?
• The *Biblical Truth* is that to know Jesus is to know God.
• The *Life Impact* is to help you grow in your knowledge of, and experience with, God.

Worldviews About Knowing God

In the secular worldview, the existence of God is either rejected or doubted. To many, the idea of a personal, all-powerful, and all-loving God is nonsense. If God exists, the deity is more like a force with which to align oneself than a Person who is aware of and cares for people.

In the biblical worldview, God is Spirit and He is Person. He is the Creator, Redeemer, and Sustainer. He is all-knowing, all-powerful, and present everywhere. To people who relate to Him in faith, He is Father in the best sense of the word. People can never fully comprehend God; but through personal experience with Jesus Christ, people of faith can know Him. Through His Word, they also can learn more about Him.

Word Study: *Know*

Just as English has several words for various shades of knowing, so does New Testament Greek. Two of the most common ones are *ginosko* and *oida.* Both words are found in the Focal Passage. Generally *ginosko* is used to describe knowledge based on experience, especially when it concerns knowing God or Christ. This is especially true in John's Gospel. This is how *ginosko* is used in John 14:7 and 9 in our Focal Passage, where it refers to personal knowledge of Jesus and of

God. The word in verses 4-5 is *oida*. There *oida* refers to the knowledge of the way that Jesus had tried to teach them. One thing is for sure: Knowing God by personal experience is given higher priority than knowing other people or things, or even knowing about God.

❖ *Search the Scriptures*

On His last night before the crucifixion, Jesus told His disciples He was going to prepare a place for them in His Father's house. He claimed to be the only way to the Father. He told them that whoever had seen Him had seen the Father. He promised they would do greater works as they lived and prayed in His name.

Provision for the Future (John 14:1-4)

*What troubled the hearts of the disciples? How could believing in God and Jesus help? What were His **Father's house** and the many **mansions**? How did Jesus explain why He was leaving? What promises did He make about their future?*

Verses 1-4: Let not your heart be troubled: ye believe in God, believe also in me. ²In my Father's house are many mansions: if it were not so, I would have told you. I go to prepare a place for you. ³And if I go and prepare a place for you, I will come again, and receive you unto myself; that where I am, there ye may be also. ⁴And whither I go ye know, and the way ye know. notes

Jesus had told them two things that **troubled** their hearts. He told them that He was going away and that they could not follow Him until later (13:33,36). He also had predicted that all of them would be offended by Him that night (Mark 14:27), and He had said that Simon Peter would deny Him (John 13:38). No wonder they were **troubled.** The Greek word is *tarassestho*. The same word is found near the end of John 14, "Peace I leave with you, my peace I give unto you, not as the world giveth, give I unto you. Let not your heart be troubled, neither let it be afraid" (v. 27). There are many causes for the troubled hearts of people in our world. Jesus' words come as a welcomed assurance. We can exchange our troubled hearts for the peace that He gives.

Ye believe is *pisteuete,* a word found twice in verse 1. The form of the verb used can be either indicative or imperative. The *King James Version* takes the first to be indicative (a statement of fact) and the

ye believe in God

Believe also in me

second to be imperative (a command); **ye believe in God, believe also in me.** The *New International Version* and *the Holman Christian Standard Bible* take both as imperatives: "Trust in God; trust also in me," and "Believe in God; believe also in Me." In either case, this is a call for faith. Faith in God and faith in Christ go together.

The promise of John 14:2-3 is among the most cherished in the Bible. It is a standard passage for funerals, but we need to cling to its assurance every day. For one thing, this promise assures us that this life is not the end. Those who know Christ will be taken to heaven. Secular people in our day either believe in an afterlife in which all will share, or they believe that death is the end for human life—beyond death is only darkness and nothingness.

The Bible does not go into great detail in describing heaven, but what it tells us brings peace to our troubled hearts. Jesus began by saying, **In my Father's house are many mansions.** Throughout John 14:1-14, Jesus referred to God as His **Father.** Not everyone responds positively to this comparison of God to a father, for some have had bad experiences with earthly fathers. However, for the rest of us, this is a powerful way to bring to our minds and hearts the sense of love and security we associate with the word. Jesus called heaven His **Father's house.** In it, He stated, **are many mansions.**

Mansions translates *monai.* This word is from the verb *meno,* which means "to dwell" or "to abide." Thus these are "dwelling places" (NRSV, HCSB) in the **Father's house.** Some translations have "rooms" (NIV, CEV). Whether we will find it to be rooms in the Father's house or separate dwelling places in His heaven, the point is clear—there is room enough for all. Wherever and whatever it is, we will be with our Heavenly Father.

The disciples were troubled because Jesus had told them He was going away. Then He explained why He was going away. **I go to prepare a place for you.** What a journey He took to do this! His journey led Him on the next day to the cross, where He suffered and died for the sins of the world. There would be no heaven without this atonement for our sins. His journey led Him into the tomb and then out of it on the first day of the week. His journey led to the right hand of the Father where He is interceding for us. His journey will lead Him back to finish God's redemptive plan. The words **I will come again, and receive you unto myself** refer to His second coming for all His people, but it also applies to His coming at death for each believer.

In a way, the pioneer Daniel Boone illustrated what Jesus did and does for us. Boone and his family lived in western North Carolina. He heard of a beautiful area now known as the Bluegrass area of Kentucky. He also heard of a pass through the high mountain range, a pass that the Indians used. So Boone and some companions set out to find this passage and this rich land, intending to go back and bring his family to it. Finally he found the Cumberland Gap and went into Kentucky. A road called the Wilderness Road was carved out along the route he had followed. Then he went back and led his family and others over the trail, through the Cumberland Gap, into the new land. Jesus is the pioneer of our salvation who went ahead of us by way of the cross and resurrection. But He does not leave us behind. He will come back to lead us through the valley of the shadow of death into heaven.

What will heaven be like? The important emphasis in the Bible is that believers will be with the Lord forever. His promise is **where I am, there ye may be also.**

Jesus then said to them, **Whither I go ye know, and the way ye know.** This led to a question by Thomas, which in turn provided Jesus the opportunity to make one of His strongest claims for Himself.

Access to the Father (John 14:5-6)

*What do we know about Thomas? In what sense is Jesus **the way, the truth, and the life**?*

Verses 5-6: **Thomas saith unto him, Lord, we know not whither thou goest; and how can we know the way?** [6]**Jesus saith unto him, I am the way, the truth, and the life: no man cometh unto the Father, but by me.**

The Gospel of John gives us personal insights into several of the twelve, including **Thomas.** He speaks three times in this Gospel. When Jesus made clear, over the objections of His disciples, that He was going to Bethany to help Mary and Martha after the death of Lazarus, Thomas showed a fatalistic courage by saying, "Let us also go, that we may die with him" (11:16). John 14:5 is the second episode. Here Thomas showed the kind of honesty also displayed in the most familiar of the incidents involving him. John 20:24-29 is the account that earned him the nickname "doubting Thomas." On each of these occasions, Jesus dealt with the honest questions and doubts of this earnest disciple.

Jesus had said that the disciples knew where He was going and the way. Thomas stated what the others were probably thinking: **Lord, we know not whither thou goest; and how can we know the way?** Thomas and no doubt the others were uncertain about Jesus' destination, and they did not know how to get there. Many of Jesus' most famous and memorable sayings were spoken in response to questions. This is no exception, for it set the stage for one of the "I am" statements in John's Gospel.

The way is used in the Bible of *the way of God* and *the way to God*. Jesus claimed to be the only way to know and to serve God. He not only shows us the way, He is the way. Jesus claimed, **No man cometh unto the Father, but by me.** Many people object to this claim. Most people believe there are many ways to God. Some ways are religious, based on one of the world's great religions or on one of the many religious cults and sects. Some people put their trust in living a good life. Others trust in mystical experiences. But the secular worldview assumes that one religion is as good as another, although many secular people believe that no religion is better than all religions or than any religion in particular.

How could Jesus claim to be the only way to God? Knowing God in time and eternity is not possible for humans to achieve by any means of their own. The only way to God is the way God has provided by His hand of love reaching down from heaven to sinful humanity. He did that in Jesus Christ.

The Greeks used the word **truth** much as we do. It means what is true versus what is false, or what is real versus what is unreal. The Hebrews added two ideas to these meanings of **truth.** For one thing, it means to be faithful and trustworthy. Second, it is personified in God Himself. Thus when Jesus said that He is **the truth,** all four meanings come into play. He is true, not false; genuine, not unreal; faithful, not unfaithful; and God, not man alone. Ultimate truth is revealed and made possible in Jesus Christ. He is "full of grace and truth" (1:14). Jesus said, "Ye shall know the truth, and the truth shall make you free" (8:32). Many quote this verse as meaning that a good education will set people free from ignorance. That has some truth in it, but Jesus was speaking of a different liberation and a different truth. Following Him faithfully is the truth that sets us free from sin (8:31-32). The tragedy is that many are face to face with the truth; yet like Pilate, they ask, "What is truth?" (18:38). **The truth** of which Jesus spoke is a person, not a concept. We know the truth when we know God through His Son Jesus Christ.

Life, like **truth,** is used many times in John's Gospel. Often the word *zoe* is found with the word *aionios* ("eternal"). The important thing about this life is that it is real life, not mere existence. Just because someone is alive physically does not ensure that the person has the life that Jesus is and offers. It is the opposite not only of death but also of merely existing. Jesus offers real life. It is abundant life. Jesus said, "I am come that they might have life, and that they might have it more abundantly" (10:10). Abundant and eternal life is also everlasting life. Endless existence without this life is the biblical definition of hell, or the second death. Christ enables us to come alive when we trust Him, and He extends this life forever.

Everyone is interested in life. Those who want to really live need to find that life by knowing God the Father through Jesus Christ His Son. God sent His Son to reveal the Father and to provide "a new and living way" to have access to God (Heb. 10:20). Jesus and Jesus alone is **the way, the truth, and the life: no man cometh unto the Father, but by** Him. "Neither is there salvation in any other: for there is none other name under heaven given among men, whereby we must be saved" (Acts 4:12).

Revelation of the Father (John 14:7-11)

What did Philip's request indicate about his lack of understanding? What did Jesus mean by saying that anyone who had seen Him had seen the Father? How does this passage contribute to the doctrine of the incarnation? Greek term means to know by experience

Verses 7-11: If ye had known me, ye should have <u>known</u> my Father also: and from henceforth ye know him, and have seen him. [8]Philip saith unto him, Lord, show us the Father, and it sufficeth us. [9]Jesus saith unto him, Have I been so long time with you, and yet hast thou not known me, Philip? he that hath seen me hath seen the Father; and how sayest thou then, Show us the Father? [10]Believest thou not that I am in the Father, and the Father in me? the words that I speak unto you I speak not of myself: but the Father that dwelleth in me, he doeth the works. [11]Believe me that I am in the Father, and the Father in me: or else believe me for the very works' sake.

Jesus followed up on verse 6 by implying that the disciples had not really known Him until then. "Really to know him is to know His Father.

God wants to be known

Up till now all has been preparation. They have not really come to the full knowledge of Jesus and His significance. But from now on it is to be different."[1] Jesus expressed confidence that now they had **known** and **seen** the Father. *wanted something tangible to strengthen his faith*

A request from Philip called the assumption of verse 7 in question. Jesus had assumed that they had seen God, but Philip requested that Jesus **show** them **the Father.** If He did this, Philip said, they would be satisfied. Philip may have had in mind the Old Testament teaching that no one could see the full glory of God and live (Ex. 33:20). This candid request, like the question of Thomas, indicated that the disciples still had not reached the maturity of faith they needed. Jesus responded by asking Philip if he had been with Him such a long time and still did not know Him. Then Jesus spoke some of His most revealing words in verse 9: **He that hath seen me hath seen the Father.**

This is one of the strongest statements of the Christian doctrine of the incarnation. It ranks along with John 1:14 and Hebrews 1:1-3 in declaring that the eternal God of the universe revealed Himself to humanity in Jesus. He is the Word who became flesh, the Word in whom God most fully revealed Himself. He is the Son of God and the express image of Him. In references to Jesus' relationship to the Father, the Bible does not use *son* in the biological sense of the word but in the Hebrew sense of a son's likeness to his father. In the Jewish life of that day, a son's objective was to be like his father. He often had a physical resemblance. He often did the same kind of work. He tried to reflect the values of his father. Therefore, when you met a man's son, you in essence also had met his father. When we come to know the Son of God, we come to know the Father.

Verses 10-11 speak of two areas of similarity: **words** and **works.** Jesus said that the *words* He spoke were not His; they were the Father's. The *works* of Jesus were not His; they were the Father's. This means that God revealed Himself in the things that Jesus said and did. Christians believe that only in Jesus Christ does God fully reveal Himself. Many people claim to believe in a god or gods, but they base their idea of God on something other than Jesus Christ. We believe that what we know of God is what we see and hear in the life, death, and resurrection of Jesus Christ. Some people say, "I believe Jesus is the Son of God because He is so like God." But the New Testament teaches us to say, "What I believe about God is what He has revealed of Himself in His Son Jesus." In other words, Jesus is the starting place for knowing God.

Jesus answer not a sharp rebuke — a gentle question

If you want to know God, you can know Him by knowing Jesus. If you want to know how God feels about something, read in the Gospels what Jesus said or did about it. How does God feel about sin and sinners? Read Jesus' words condemning sin and the stories of His compassion in seeking sinners. Above all, stand at the cross and see how Jesus died for sinners. God's condemnation of sin and His love for sinners are revealed at the cross.

Promise of Enablement (John 14:12-14)

*In what sense can followers of Jesus do **greater works** than He did? What is involved in praying in Jesus' name?*

Verses 12-14: Verily, verily, I say unto you, He that believeth on me, the works that I do shall he do also; and greater works than these shall he do; because I go unto my Father. [13]And whatsoever ye shall ask in my name, that will I do, that the Father may be glorified in the Son. [14]If ye shall ask anything in my name, I will do it.

These verses contain two amazing promises. The first is Jesus' promise in verse 12. Jesus promised that those who believe in Him would do His **works**; in fact, He said that they would do **greater works**. What did He mean by **works**? At times this word (*erga*) was used of the miracles of Jesus (7:21). At other times the word was used of deeds other than miracles. The word may be used in the singular of an individual act or of the sum total of Jesus' earthly life (17:4) or in the plural of more than one of His deeds (15:24). Thus, when applied to His followers, **works** can refer either to miracles or to Christlike deeds of service (see Eph. 2:10).

Greater works are "not necessarily greater miracles and not greater spiritual works in quality, but greater in quantity."[2] In other words, Jesus was not promising that believers would do greater acts of mercy than He did; instead, He was saying that many believers used by His Spirit could do more deeds of service than He could do alone during His earthly ministry. Jesus was limited to one time and place. Now His Spirit works through countless followers all over the world. Keep in mind that these are still His works, which are dependent on the power and presence of His Spirit. Jesus continues His work in and through the lives of all who know Him.

The second promise is closely related to the first promise. The power to do the greater works comes from the Lord through prayer in *notes*

His name. Jesus promised to do whatever believers **ask in** His **name.** He reinforced this by saying, **If ye shall ask anything in my name, I will do it.** The purpose of such prayers and their answers is **that the Father may be glorified in the Son.** What does it mean to pray in Jesus' name? It surely means more than adding to our prayers the words "in Jesus' name." We must be living in His name to truly pray in His name. Living in His name is allowing Him to do the greater works through us—works that glorify God by meeting human needs in the name of Jesus. When we are asking for something needed to do what God has called us to do for His glory, we can ask in confidence that He will give us what we need to fulfill His will.

❖ *Spiritual Transformations*

In "Search the Scriptures," we have seen that Jesus made some strong claims for Himself. He went before us to prepare places for us in the house of our Father. He is the way, the truth, and the life. Whoever has seen Jesus has seen the Father. His two amazing promises were that believers could do greater works than He did and that whatever such people ask in His name they will receive.

The "Life Impact" is that you grow in your knowledge of, and experience with, God. This involves a growing faith and relationship with His Son, Jesus Christ. This kind of experience involves more than knowing more about God; it requires that we know Him personally and grow in that relationship. "You will never be satisfied to just know *about* God. Knowing God only comes through experience as He reveals Himself to you."[3]

In what ways are you seeking to grow in your knowledge of God?

_____

What has been your experience in praying in Jesus' name?

_____

Prayer of Commitment: Lord, help me to know You better and to live and to pray in the name of Jesus. Amen.

[1]Leon Morris, *The Gospel According to John,* in the New International Commentary on the New Testament [Grand Rapids: William B. Eerdmans Publishing Company, 1971], 642.

[2]A. T. Robertson, *Word Pictures in the New Testament,* vol. 5 [Nashville: Broadman Press, 1932], 251.

[3]Henry T. Blackaby and Claude V. King *Experiencing God: Knowing and Doing the Will of God* [Nashville: Lifeway Press, 1990], 57.

BEING PRODUCTIVE

Bible Passage: John 15:1-17
Key Verse: John 15:5

❖ *Significance of the Lesson*

• The *Theme* of this lesson is that, as a result of an abiding relationship with Jesus, His disciples will bear fruit.

• The *Life Question* this lesson seeks to address is, What does Jesus expect of me?

• The *Biblical Truth* is that because of their ongoing close relationship with Him, Jesus expects His followers to be productive for Him and enables them to be so.

• The *Life Impact* is to help you be productive for Christ.

Productivity

The secular worldview of productivity has no place for moral and spiritual productivity. To secular people, productivity means using their skills and intellect to obtain social and professional status, to accumulate material things, and to achieve earthly success. They see their value in terms of what they can produce through their work.

The biblical worldview defines productivity in terms of a personal relationship with Christ and the moral and spiritual fruit flowing from that relationship. He empowers those who abide in Him to live in such a way as to glorify God by their attitudes and actions.

Word Study: *Abide, Abideth, Continue, Remain*

The word *meno* is found 11 times in the Focal Passage—three times in verse 4; twice in verses 7 and 10; and once in verses 5,6,9, and 16. In the *King James Version*, this word is translated by the four English words listed above. The word literally means "to stay," in the sense of living, dwelling, or lodging somewhere. Figuratively it means to abide, continue, or remain in someone or something. The most characteristic use of the word in this lesson is to abide in Christ as He abides in believers and His words abide in them. This is the same kind of relationship a vine has with its branches. This abiding also includes abiding in Jesus' love as He abided in the Father's love.

❖ *Search the Scriptures*

After claiming to be the true Vine, Jesus compared people to branches that need to abide in Him. The result of this union is to bear fruit. Jesus called on believers to abide in His love, to love one another, and to go forth in His name.

Remain in Jesus (John 15:1-4)

*Why did Jesus call Himself **the true vine**? In what sense does the Father cleanse the branches? What does it mean to **abide in** Christ?*

Verses 1-4: I am the true vine, and my Father is the husbandman. [2]Every branch in me that beareth not fruit he taketh away: and every branch that beareth fruit, he purgeth it, that it may bring forth more fruit. [3]Now ye are clean through the word which I have spoken unto you. [4]Abide in me, and I in you. As the branch cannot bear fruit of itself, except it abide in the vine; no more can ye, except ye abide in me.

I am the true ("real," NEB) **vine.** Here is another of the "I am" statements of Jesus in John's Gospel. All of these are claims to a unique relationship with God, and each bears witness to Jesus as the only source of life abundant and eternal. Each, however, has its own distinctive message.

Jesus lived and taught in a rural society. Thus He used the things people of His day understood. Growing grapes was a crucial part of first-century life. The grapes provided food and drink for the people. Successfully growing vines that bore fruit was vitally important. For a branch, abiding in the vine was a source of life and sustenance.

The vine was important also because it had become a symbol for the Jewish people. It is pictured on some of the coins of the era of the Maccabees (second century before Christ). A huge golden vine was also on the front of the holy place in the temple. The Old Testament often referred to Israel as a vine or vineyard, but each of these references pictures the sinful failure of Israel to bear the fruit God expected.

Isaiah 5:1-7 is typical of these passages. God had done His part to ensure that the vineyard would bear good fruit, but instead it brought forth wild grapes. Hosea exclaimed, "Israel is an empty vine" (10:1). Jeremiah recorded this question of God for Israel, "I had planted thee a noble vine, wholly a right seed: how then art thou turned into a degenerate plant of a strange vine unto me?" (2:21). Psalm 80 tells how God called a vine out of Egypt, blessed it, and then brought judgment on it. The psalmist prayed for the Lord's mercy (vv. 8-19).

Many first-century Jews trusted in their physical heritage as descendants of Abraham as all they needed to be right with God. We see this in passages such as Matthew 3:9 and John 8:39. Jesus was telling them that they should not trust in belonging to Israel; only in belonging to Him is there life and a right relationship with God.

All of this is in the background of Jesus' words, **I am the true vine.** "It is as if Jesus said, 'You think that because you belong to the nation of Israel you are a branch in the true vine of God. . . . But it is not the nation who is the true vine. The nation is a degenerate vine, as all your prophets saw. It is I who am the true vine. It is not the fact that you are a Jew which will save you. The only thing that can save you is to have an intimate living fellowship and belief with *me*, for I am the vine of God, and you must be branches joined to me.'"[1]

My Father is the husbandman ("gardener," NIV; "vineyard keeper," HCSB) indicates that the vine belongs to God, and He expects it to bear fruit. God does His part to make this possible, but a vine has two kinds of branches—those that bear fruit and those that do not. God **taketh away** ("removes," HCSB) the unfruitful branches (see v. 6 for their fate). In the sentence, **Every branch that beareth fruit, he purgeth it, that it may bring forth more fruit,** the word **purgeth** is *kathairei*, which normally means "to cleanse." It is the same word Jesus used when He said to all the apostles except Judas that they were "clean" (13:10-11). Here the word means "he prunes" (NASB). There is a play on words in the Greek between the words for "takes away" and "prunes," *airei* and *kathairei*. The former means to "cut off"; the latter means to "cut away."

In John 15:2 Jesus did not elaborate on what is involved in this pruning of the lives of fruitful followers. Many Bible students think that He was referring to the disciplining of the Father in the lives of His children (see Heb. 12:6-11). This passage in Hebrews points out that being disciplined is not pleasant, but it is one evidence that we belong to the Father. Closely related to this is the process of testing His people that God sometimes allows for our long-range good. Notice that the purpose of this cleansing is **that it may bring forth more fruit.**

As Jesus did in John 13:10-11, He reassured the disciples they were already **clean through the word** He had **spoken unto** them. As at the foot washing, they did not need a full cleansing, but they needed occasional washings; here also they needed occasional pruning by the Father. Since He is the keeper of the vineyard, He knows and does what is best for the vines to bear fruit.

Abide in me, and I in you is the basic lesson of the relationship of believers to Jesus as **the true vine.** Several important truths are either spelled out or implied by this description of our relationship with Him. Since the word *meno* basically means "to dwell," this is one way of saying that believers dwell with and in the Lord and He with and in them. This close personal relationship is pictured as being like the relationship of a vine and its branches.

The word for **branches** in this passage is *klema,* which refers to a branch of a vine. This is different from *klados,* which refers to the branch of a tree. The relation of a tree branch to the trunk is not so close as that of a vine branch to the vine. The branch of a vine is more like an integral part of the vine. "He is the Vine, not the trunk over against the branches; the latter are *in him* as part of the plant. The image is feasible prior to the death and resurrection of Jesus, in terms of fellowship and discipleship, but its full meaning is possible only on the basis of the Easter event and the sending of the Holy Spirit. So understood it is remarkably similar to the figure of Christ as the Body that includes the Church."[2]

Another meaning of **abide** is "to continue" or "to remain." Thus this relationship with the true Vine is not short but permanent. Those who come to know Christ continue to know Him and to grow in Him. There is constancy to this relationship when it is real.

An important meaning of this relationship is that it is fruitful. The purpose of the vine and its branches is to bear fruit: **As the branch cannot bear fruit of itself, except it abide in the vine, no more can ye, except ye abide in me.** A vine without branches cannot bear fruit. The Lord is dependent on His followers to fulfill His purpose. But we are even more dependent on Him. An unattached branch is not able to bear fruit, nor is it able to sustain life. It is dead and unfruitful.

Be Productive (John 15:5-8)

*What is the **fruit**? How is it produced? How can **much fruit** be produced? What kinds of people are like the fruitless branches? How is prayer involved in this process? How does this differ from secular meanings of productivity?*

Verses 5-8: **I am the vine, ye are the branches: He that abideth in me, and I in him, the same bringeth forth much fruit: for without me ye can do nothing.** [6]**If a man abide not in me, he is cast forth as a branch, and is withered; and men gather them, and cast them into the fire, and they are burned.** [7]**If ye abide in me, and my words abide in you, ye shall ask what ye will, and it shall be done unto you.** [8]**Herein is my Father glorified, that ye bear much fruit; so shall ye be my disciples.**

Verse 5 reinforces the basic message. Jesus is **the vine and** believers **are the branches.** When believers abide in Christ and He abides in them, **the same bringeth forth much fruit.** *Karpos* **(fruit)** is found throughout the passage. It is in verses 2,4,5,8, and 16. It is used with the word *phero* **(bear).** *Karpos* often refers to literal fruit, but it also is used at times in a figurative way. Most often the figurative meaning has to do with good qualities of life. The most familiar of these is Paul's contrast between the works of the flesh and the fruit of the Spirit (Gal. 5:19-23); however, similar meanings are found in Philippians 1:11 and James 3:18. The fruit of a person who lives in union with Christ is Christlike living. Such fruit is evidence of our union with Christ.

Another meaning of **fruit** is winning others to Christ. This seems to be Paul's meaning in Romans 1:13. Paul wrote the Romans that he wanted to visit Rome that he might have some fruit among them also. These words were spoken in a context about boldly telling the good news (Rom. 1:14-16). This is probably the meaning of **fruit** in John 15:16.

Verses 5 and 8 add the word **much** to **fruit.** F. B. Meyer observed: "Nowhere does the Lord contemplate a *little fruit.* A berry here and there! A thin bunch of sour, unripened grapes! Yet it is too true that many believers yield no more than this."[3] The Lord's will is that believers be fruitful and that they bear much fruit.

How is this possible? It is not possible through our own efforts. Verses 4 and 5 emphasize that we cannot bear fruit unless we abide in Christ. Jesus said, **Without me ye can do nothing.**

Verse 6 returns to those mentioned in verse 2—those who were cut off because they did not bear fruit. Two observations about this statement are needed. For one thing, those cut off were not condemned for bearing evil fruit but for bearing no good fruit. Some people bear evil fruit (Matt. 7:15-20), but others simply fail to bear the kind of positive fruit that grows out of a vital relationship with the Lord.

The second observation is that we should not press the analogy to teach that saved people can become lost again. This conclusion might be drawn if every point in the parable or analogy is pressed for meaning. The point is that fruitless branches are useless and fit only for burning. It is like Jesus' teaching that believers are the salt of the earth, but if the salt has lost its saltiness (as first-century salt could do), it is "good for nothing" (Matt. 5:13). Some, such as Herschel Hobbs, believed that this verse was not a reference to hell fire.[4] Even if it is, the dead branches might refer to people who never had a real relationship to the Lord but just appeared to have such. No doubt Judas was in the mind of the other apostles as they thought back about that night. He appeared to have been a disciple, but his actions called that possibility into doubt. There are too many references in the New Testament to the security of true believers to deny it here (see, for example, 10:27-29). We must recognize that anyone who professes to be a Christian and fails to bear *much* fruit for the Lord is in a serious moral and spiritual condition.

Verse 7 refers to prayer. This is one of the themes that run throughout the teachings in the upper room (see 14:13-14). Verse 7 identifies those who **abide in** Christ as those in whom His **words abide.** When this is true, Jesus promised, **ye shall ask what ye will, and it shall be done unto you.** This is similar to the promise about praying in His name. Prayer is not a blank check for getting what we want; it is conditioned on our abiding in Christ and His words abiding in us. The ones who are in Him are seeking His will.

Another fact about prayer is that abiding in Christ is a prayerful relationship. Prayer is not primarily petition but communion. The condition of abiding in Christ assumes a vital union expressed in prayer.

Verse 8 adds two more emphases. One is that God is **glorified** in the lives of those who **bear much fruit.** Second, Jesus said, **so shall ye be my disciples.** This is sometimes taken to mean that we come to be His disciples by bearing fruit. That misses the point. We do not bear fruit and then become attached to the vine. We bear fruit because we are abiding in Christ. Thus the last part of verse 8 means that by bearing much fruit and glorifying the Father, we show ourselves to be His disciples—"and so prove to be My disciples" (NASB); "showing your-selves to be my disciples" (NIV).

The heading for verses 5-8 in this lesson is "Be Productive." What is the difference between being productive as a Christian and being productive by secular standards? Industry defines being productive as producing products, especially in abundance. It is closely related to being profitable. In individual lives being productive means bringing home a paycheck or doing something the person considers useful. Because of this, homemakers and retirees often feel they are useless and unproductive. People who lose their health often feel the same way. Jesus defined productivity in terms of moral and spiritual fruit. Each believer—homemakers, the physically challenged, retirees included—can bear this kind of fruit.

When John Milton, the great English writer of *Paradise Lost,* was 44 years old, he went totally blind. Being a writer, this seemed a deadly blow to his productivity. He wrote a poem entitled "On His Blindness." In his poem he expressed his initial fear that his one talent had now become useless. But patience taught him that although thousands serve God as they fulfill missions over land and ocean, "they also serve who only stand and wait."[5]

Remain in Jesus' Love (John 15:9-11)

What does it mean to abide in Jesus' love? How can believers come to share Christ's joy?

Verses 9-11: **As the Father hath loved me, so have I loved you: continue ye in my love. [10]If ye keep my commandments, ye shall abide in my love; even as I have kept my Father's commandments, and abide in his love. [11]These things have I spoken unto you, that my joy might remain in you, and that your joy might be full.**

The Father's **love** for the Son is the basis for His love for His follow-ers. The relation of Father and Son thus is love. "God is love" (1 John 4:8). In the same way, Jesus said that He **loved** the disciples. He loved them with the same love with which He was loved.

Continue is the same word translated "abide" in earlier verses. Abiding in Christ means to abide in His love. Doing so should enable us to relax and entrust ourselves to Him. We need not worry or fear if we abide in the love of the Son of God. This love assures us of our initial acceptance and of our continuing security in His hands.

Abiding in His love is demonstrated by keeping the Lord's **commandments.** The wording can be misunderstood. Jesus was not saying that we become His disciples by keeping His commandments any more than He was saying that He abided in the Father's love by keeping His commandments. Rather, His point was that those who abide in divine love show this by obeying divine commandments.

Closely related to love is **joy.** Thus within a few verses we have the first three of Paul's list of the fruit of the Spirit (Gal. 5:22): love, joy, peace (14:27; 15:9-10,11). Jesus spoke of **my joy.** What was His joy? Two verses illustrate His joy. After Jesus led the woman of Samaria to take the water of life, Jesus was asked to eat something. He replied, "I have meat to eat that ye know not of. . . . My meat is to do the will of him that sent me, and to finish his work" (4:32,34). Hebrews 12:2 says that Jesus "for the joy that was set before him endured the cross, despising the shame, and is set down at the right hand of the throne of God." Unsaved people often think of Jesus as a killjoy. Actually He is a joy-giver. His joy is dependent only upon doing the will of the Father. Such joy is inward and lasting, but it also leads to true happiness.

Martin Luther, the great 16th-century reformer of the church, was in a mood of melancholy. His wife appeared at breakfast dressed in black as if she were in mourning. He asked, "Who is dead?" She replied, "Do you not know? God is dead." Luther reproved her for her blasphemy: "How can God be dead? He is eternal." Her answer must have stung: "Yes, but from the way you are cast down, one would think that God must be dead."[6]

Abiding in Christ involves abiding in His love and experiencing His joy. His objective is that His **joy might remain in** us, **and that** our **joy might be full.** Such love and joy are part of the fruit that comes from abiding in Him.

Love One Another (John 15:12-17)

Why is loving one another so vital? What does it mean to be Jesus' friends? In what sense have we chosen Him and He chosen us? What is the meaning of fruit in verse 16?

Verses 12-17: This is my commandment, That ye love one another, as I have loved you. [13]Greater love hath no man than this, that a man lay down his life for his friends. [14]Ye are my friends, if ye do whatsoever I command you. [15]Henceforth I call you not

servants; for the servant knoweth not what his lord doeth: but I have called you friends; for all things that I have heard of my Father I have made known unto you. [16]Ye have not chosen me, but I have chosen you, and ordained you, that ye should go and bring forth fruit, and that your fruit should remain: that whatsoever ye shall ask of the Father in my name, he may give it you. [17]These things I command you, that ye love one another.

Earlier on that night Jesus had said: "A new commandment I give unto you, That ye love one another; as I have loved you, that ye also love one another. By this shall all men know that ye are my disciples, if ye have love one to another" (13:34-35). This same exhortation is in verses 12 and 17. It is based on God's divine love for us: **Love one another, as I have loved you.**

The supreme act of love is laying down one's life for others. Verse 13 expressed a saying familiar in ancient times, but Jesus did more than die to rescue others from some earthly danger. He died to save us from our sins (Rom. 5:6-8). Jesus' death is what enables us to be called His **friends.** This is what He called His followers in verses 13-15. What does it mean to be a friend of Jesus?

For one thing, being Jesus' friends means that we have the assurance that God is for us, not against us. We abide in His love. Second, it means that we **do whatsoever** He commands us to do. Third, it means a kind of intimacy in which He shares Himself and His plans with us. Jesus said that He did not call them **servants** but **friends.** We are of course servants, just as Jesus Himself was the ultimate Servant. This was the lesson of the foot washing in chapter 13. Yet we have a more personal relationship with Him than a master does with his slaves. The Roman emperors had special groups called "friends of Caesar." How much more wonderful it is to be one of the friends of Christ!

Verse 16 is a key verse that makes three main points: First, Jesus told the apostles, **Ye have not chosen me, but I have chosen you.** Each of them could recall when the Lord had first said, "Come, follow Me." This is also true of each believer. Each is chosen for salvation and service. But someone may say, "I thought I chose the Lord." We do choose to follow Him, but this choice is possible only because He first chose us. Israel was a chosen nation, but they made the mistake of thinking of choice primarily as a privilege rather than a responsibility.

When the Lord chooses us, He chooses us for mission in His name. Thus the second point is found in the middle part of the verse. Jesus said, **I have . . . ordained you, that ye should go and bring forth fruit. Ordained** is *etheka*, which means "appointed" (NIV, HCSB, NASB, NKJV, NRSV, REB). Jesus' words, **that ye should go and bring forth fruit,** seem to point to a different kind of **fruit** than is found in earlier verses of John 15. This is the kind of enduring fruit that comes when believers go forth on mission for the Lord. Thus Jesus probably had in mind people who are won to Him as His disciples go forth in His name. The fruit of a Christian should be another Christian.

The third point in verse 16 is the assurance that those who go forth on the Lord's mission are acting in His name and in His place. Therefore, they can be sure that **the Father** will **give** them whatever they need to act in the name of Jesus.

❖ *Spiritual Transformations*

In "Search the Scriptures," we have seen several teachings. Believers abide in Christ as branches abide in the vine. Those who abide in Him bear much fruit. Those who abide in Him abide in His love and experience His joy. They reflect Jesus' love by loving one another and by going forth to bear lasting fruit.

The *Life Impact* of being productive can be defined in three ways: bearing the fruit of the Spirit, loving one another, and bearing the lasting fruit of faithful witness for Christ.

Read about the fruit of the Spirit in Galatians 5:22-23. Which fruit do you most need? _____

How much lasting fruit of new converts has the Lord won through your witness for Him? _____

Prayer of Commitment: Lord, help us to so abide in You that we bear fruit for the glory of the Father. Amen.

[1]William Barclay, *The Gospel of John,* vol. 2, second edition, in The Daily Study Bible [Philadelphia: The Westminster Press, 1956], 201-202.

[2]George R. Beasley-Murray, *John,* in the Word Biblical Commentary, vol. 36 [Waco: Word Books, Publishers, 1987], 272.

[3]F. B. Meyer, *Gospel of John* [London: Marshall, Morgan & Scott, 1956], 263.

[4]Herschel H. Hobbs, *The Gospel of John: Invitation to Life* [Nashville: Convention Press, 1988], 263.

[5]John Milton, as quoted in *Masterpieces of Religious Verse,* edited by James Dalton Morrison [New York: Harper & Brothers Publishers, 1948], 1325.

[6]Leonard Griffith, *The Eternal Legacy from an Upper Room* [New York: Harper & Row, Publishers, 1963], 132.

RECEIVING THE HOLY SPIRIT

Background Passage: John 14:15-18; 15:26–16:16
Focal Passage: John 14:16-17; 15:26-27; 16:5-15
Key Verses: John 14:16-17

❖ *Significance of the Lesson*

• The *Theme* of this lesson is that the Holy Spirit continues the work of Christ in believers and in the world.
• The *Life Question* this lesson seeks to address is, How does God relate to me day by day?
• The *Biblical Truth* is that Jesus has sent the Holy Spirit to live in believers and to continue Jesus' work in the world.
• The *Life Impact* is to help you allow the Holy Spirit to continue Christ's work through you.

Worldviews on the Holy Spirit

In the secular worldview, the concept of God's Spirit living in people to give them strength and guidance is laughable and irrelevant to real life. Secular people believe that life is lived in a person's own strength. If a process is involved in decision-making, it is one of the intellect, which is informed by one's own intellect and sometimes by advice from individuals who are utilized as resource persons. Truth is considered relative and is found in many philosophies. Moral standards are determined by what brings pleasure or success. Some secular people turn to a false kind of spirituality that is totally different from the biblical view.

In the biblical worldview, the Holy Spirit convicts people of their sins and points them to Jesus. When people place their faith in Jesus Christ, the Holy Spirit comes into their lives. The Spirit abides with believers, moves them toward moral and spiritual maturity, strengthens them in times of need, and empowers them as witnesses and servants of Christ in the world.

Jesus' Teachings About the Holy Spirit in John 14–16

The final teachings of Jesus in John's Gospel begin with Jesus' telling the disciples that He was going away. They were disturbed by this announcement, and Jesus sought to help them in several ways. For one thing, He told them that He was going to prepare a place for them and that He would return to take them with Him. For another thing, He emphasized that His Spirit would continue to be with them and make them sufficient for every situation. These teachings about the Spirit are not found in one block of verses in the upper room discourse but are interspersed throughout the three chapters in 14:16-17,26; 15:26-27; and 16:5-15.

Word Study: *Comforter*

In the teachings of His last night, Jesus referred to the Holy Spirit as *parakletos* (John 14:16,26; 15:26; 16:7). Most believe that this word is from *parakaleo*, which means to "call along side to help." *Parakletos* was used by the Greeks to refer to a person who stands with someone in a court setting. We can see this meaning in 1 John 2:1, where the title Paraclete is used of the glorified Jesus who is our advocate in heaven. Passages such as John 15:26-27 and 16:8-11 also have a legal background. The other uses of the word seem to have a more general meaning. Translators struggle to find the best English word to capture its essence. Among these are "Comforter" (KJV), "Advocate" (REB, NEB, NRSV), "Helper" (NKJV, NASB), and "Counselor" (NIV, HCSB). Some simply use the transliterated Greek word "Paraclete," feeling that no one English word captures its meaning (NJB). Leon Morris wrote: "It is impossible to find one English word that will cover all that the *parakletos* does."[1] Jesus made clear that He was speaking of "the Spirit of truth" (14:17; 15:26; 16:13), one of many names for "the Holy Spirit" (14:26; NIV, HCSB).

❖ *Search the Scriptures*

Jesus promised to send another paraclete who would abide with His followers after He was gone. The Spirit would bear testimony to Jesus and enable His followers to be witnesses. Jesus said that unless He went away, the Spirit could not come. The Spirit convicts the world of its sin. He does not call attention to Himself but glorifies Jesus. In this lesson we will focus on four specific truths about the Holy Spirit.

An Abiding Presence (John 14:16-17)

*In what sense was the Spirit **another Comforter**? What is the relation of the presence of the living Lord and the Spirit? Why did Jesus emphasize that the Spirit would abide with them? Why does the world not recognize the Spirit? How can believers know the Spirit?*

14:16-17: And I will pray the Father, and he shall give you another Comforter, that he may abide with you forever; [17]even the Spirit of truth; whom the world cannot receive, because it seeth him not, neither knoweth him: but ye know him; for he dwelleth with you, and shall be in you.

Jesus had promised His disciples that they would do greater works than He had done as the incarnate Son of God (vv. 12-14). He had called those who loved Him to keep His commandments (v. 15). How were they to be able to do this? His promise in verses 16-17 reveals His answer.

Jesus promised to ask **the Father** to **give** them **another Comforter. Another** is *allon,* which refers to another of the same kind. In other words, Jesus had done the work of a paraclete. He was with them. He convicted people of sin. He was their teacher. He bore witness to the truth. Now He was about to leave them as a physical presence, but the Father would send another like Jesus to be with them. This insight helps us understand the work of the Spirit. We can look at what Jesus did and see what the Spirit does.

Just as the unbelieving world did not recognize Jesus for who He is, so **the Spirit of truth . . . the world cannot receive.** The world recognizes as real only what it can see and know by its own limited criteria. Having no experience with the Spirit and being unable to see Him, the world denies or ignores Him. Paul wrote of how unaware of the realm of the Spirit is the natural man: "The natural man receiveth not the things of the Spirit of God: for they are foolishness unto him: neither can he know them, because they are spiritually discerned" (1 Cor. 2:14). By contrast, believers recognize the Spirit because they **know** Him through personal experience. There is a lot of talk today about "spirit" and "spirituality" that has nothing to do with the true Spirit. Those who know the Spirit of the Lord Jesus recognize Him and His work.

One of the most treasured things Jesus did for the apostles was to be with them as companion, teacher, and divine Son. Jesus emphasized that the new paraclete would **abide with** believers **forever.** Although Jesus in His incarnate form was about to leave, His Spirit was to come to be with them. Their relationship to the Spirit was not the kind of physical contact to which they had become accustomed, but it was real and true. Because of the close relation of the Spirit to the Lord Jesus, they felt His abiding presence in them and with them.

A Witness About Christ (John 15:26-27)

What is the relationship between God as Father, Son, and Spirit? Why do we speak of the Spirit as a person, not an influence? In what ways does the Spirit testify to Jesus? How does this relate to the witness of the apostles and of all believers?

15:26-27: But when the Comforter is come, whom I will send unto you from the Father, even the Spirit of truth, which proceedeth from the Father, he shall testify of me: ²⁷and ye also shall bear witness, because ye have been with me from the beginning.

In 14:16 Jesus said that He would ask the Father to send another paraclete. In 15:26 Jesus said that He would **send** the paraclete **from the Father. The Spirit of truth** is described as proceeding **from the Father.** Someone may ask, who sends the Spirit—Jesus or the Father? The answer to this and similar questions brings to mind the Christian doctrine of the Trinity. Jesus spoke of Himself and His Father as having a very close relation: "I and my Father are one" (10:30); "He that hath seen me hath seen the Father" (14:9). Yet Jesus did not claim to be the Father.

In the background to this issue is the Christian understanding of the one God as Father, Son, and Holy Spirit. This doctrine defies the rules of human logic, but it is consistent with how God has revealed Himself and how we have experienced Him. We must recognize that God is bigger than our limited abilities to fully comprehend and describe Him. When we say "one," we think of one thing in one form at one place; but the oneness of God is bigger than that. The Bible teaches us that God is Father who is always beyond us, that He sent His Son to save us, and that He abides in us by His Spirit. This biblical revelation matches how we experience God. He is the Father to whom we pray, the Son through whom we pray, and the Spirit in whom we pray. Jesus spoke of the close relation of the Father and the Son; He did the same thing for the Son and the Spirit. The work of God is the work of the Son, and the work of both is fulfilled by the presence of the unseen Spirit. Thus the Spirit is the unseen presence of God and His Son with us, in us, and among us.

Another truth about the Spirit is that He is a person, not an influence. We sometimes use the English word *spirit* to refer to an influence. The Greek word for *spirit* is *pneuma*, which is neuter. However, the gender of Greek words did not mean what we mean by the word *gender*. The word translated **he** in verse 26 is *ekeinos*, which is masculine. The language about the paraclete makes clear that the Spirit is a person.

The main point of verse 26 focuses on the work of the paraclete in bearing witness to Jesus. The word **testify** is the same as the words translated **bear witness** in verse 27. Both are forms of the word *martureo*, from which we get our word *martyr* (because a faithful witness in those days often was killed). Jesus had just described the hatred of the world for Him and predicted a similar hatred for His followers. Jesus had given faithful testimony to God in spite of such murderous hatred. The paraclete would bear faithful testimony to the continuing work of God in Jesus.

Verse 27 confirms what is consistently taught in the New Testament: The Spirit empowers and uses believers as witnesses for Christ. Verse 27 applied directly to the apostles. Jesus told them, **ye have been with me from the beginning.** When He called the twelve, He called them to be with Him (Mark 3:14). When a successor for Judas was sought, a key qualification was to have been with Jesus from the beginning (Acts 1:21-22). The apostles were a unique group of witnesses. They were eyewitnesses of Jesus' life, teachings, and resurrection. Jesus appointed them to bear witness to the truth they had seen and heard. Their testimony continues through the New Testament itself.

Jesus, however, broadened the task of witnessing to all believers with the coming of His Spirit at Pentecost. He expects believers today to be Spirit-filled witnesses. If you look up the references to being filled with the Spirit in the Book of Acts, you will find that the one thing most of these passages have in common is that they describe Spirit-filled and Spirit-led believers bearing a bold witness for Jesus Christ. This is the Lord's commission (1:8). It is what happened on Pentecost (2:4). Many of the examples in Acts were bold witnesses in the face of threats and danger. When the believers at Jerusalem were threatened, they prayed not for deliverance but for boldness to speak God's word: "And when they had prayed, the place was shaken where they were assembled together; and they were all filled with the Holy Ghost, and they spake the word of God with boldness" (4:31). Other examples are Peter (4:8), Stephen (6:5; 7:55), Philip (8:29), and Paul (13:4,9; 16:6-10).

A Convicting Messenger (John 16:5-11)

Why did Jesus tell the apostles that it was for their good that He go away? In what sense was the coming of the Spirit after Jesus' departure different from the Holy Spirit's work before Jesus' departure? What is the meaning of the word reprove? In what three areas would the Spirit reprove the world?

16:5-7: But now I go my way to him that sent me; and none of you asketh me, Whither goest thou? ⁶But because I have said these things unto you, sorrow hath filled your heart. ⁷Nevertheless I tell you the truth; It is expedient for you that I go away: for if I go not away, the Comforter will not come unto you; but if I depart, I will send him unto you.

Jesus had just warned again of the hatred of the world against Him and against the disciples (16:1-4). After this solemn warning, He told them again that He was going on His **way** to the One who had **sent** Him. Bible students often are puzzled that verse 5 says that none of the apostles asked Him where He was going. Is this not the very question that Thomas had asked Him in 14:5? How then can we explain what Jesus meant in 16:5? Two factors help us understand. For one thing, they may have already had their question answered; therefore, they no longer asked it. Second, they were much more concerned with what would happen to them than they were to know the details about where Jesus was going. Their response to the news that He was going away was that **sorrow . . . filled** their **heart.**

Notice that verse 7 begins with **nevertheless.** The words **I tell you the truth** show that Jesus wanted the disciples to pay special attention. Although the disciples felt only deep grief that Jesus was going away, He emphasized to them that going away was **expedient** for them. **Expedient** translates *sumpherei*, which means "to your advantage" (NKJV), "for your benefit" (HCSB), or "for your good" (NIV). They wondered how the Master's departure could possibly be for their benefit. Jesus explained, **If I go not away, the Comforter will not come unto you; but if I depart, I will send him unto you.**

Why did Jesus have to leave for the paraclete to come? This is a crucial question. The Bible teaches that the Holy Spirit is eternal with the Father and the Son. He was there in the beginning (Gen. 1:2). He was present in Old Testament times. And He was active in the time of Jesus. However, the Spirit could not come with full power until the redemptive work of the Son was finished through His death and resurrection. John 7:39 says that "the Holy Ghost was not yet given: because that Jesus was not yet glorified." This does not mean that the Spirit was not already at work; it means that the Spirit's full power came after the cross and the resurrection.

16:8-11: **And when he is come, he will reprove the world of sin, and of righteousness, and of judgment: [9]of sin, because they believe not on me; [10]of righteousness, because I go to my Father, and ye see me no more; [11]of judgment, because the prince of this world is judged.**

These verses deal with the work of the Spirit in **the world,** in contrast to His work among believers. The key word is the one translated **reprove.** *Elencho* had many meanings among the Greeks. In various circumstances it could mean "to shame," "to blame," "to expose," "to resist," "to expound," "to investigate," or "to convict." In this context many translations have "convict" (NKJV, NIV, HCSB, NASB). Some of the legal background of the word *parakletos* is preserved; however, instead of acting as defense attorney (as in 1 John 2:1), He acts here as prosecuting attorney and judge. The Holy Spirit acts as a convicting force in laying bare before their eyes the sins of people of the world. He pronounces inner judgment on them. Secular people might call these experiences twinges of conscience or moments of truth—and they are—but they are also the result of the convicting power of the Spirit.

Jesus mentioned three areas in which the Spirit convicts people of the world: **He will reprove the world of sin, and of righteousness, and of judgment.** All three areas are closely related. **Sin** is not something that many modern-day people are concerned about. Some make fun of anyone so old-fashioned as to still believe in sin and guilt—at least in their own lives. The word is not used in sophisticated company. Yet sin is the basic problem that lies behind all human problems. The Spirit seeks to convict each person of this truth.

The particular sin of which the Spirit convicts sinners is the sin of rejecting Jesus. He convicts **of sin,** Jesus said, **because they believe**

not on me. One of the other uses of *elencho* is in 3:20. This use comes right after John 3:16. God has offered His great love, but some reject His love. These people stand condemned already. They refuse to come to the light lest their deeds should be reproved. Many people consider sin a kind of brave rebellion against a distant deity, but it is an act of rejection against a God of great love, who gave His Son to save sinners. Those who reject that love stand condemned.

The Spirit convicts the world **of righteousness,** Jesus said, **because I go to my Father, and ye see me no more.** While Jesus was on earth, He taught and exemplified true righteousness. He showed that self-righteousness is an expression of pride that keeps people from God as much as any sin (see Luke 18:9-14). The Holy Spirit now performs that mission in human hearts all around the world.

Finally, Jesus said the Spirit would convict the world **of judgment, because the prince of this world is judged.** As Jesus predicted the cross, He said in John 12:31, "Now is the judgment of this world: now shall the prince of this world be cast out." The cross followed by the res-urrection reversed the condemnation of Jesus by the world, under the influence of Satan. The dark forces of sin and Satan declared Jesus guilty of crimes worthy of death, and they crucified Him, sealed Him in a tomb, and rejoiced in their victory over the Son of God. But God raised Jesus from the dead and showed that the cross was a great victory over sin, death, and Satan. Those who choose to follow the prince of this world are on a sinking ship. They do not need to wait until the day of judgment to discover their eternal destiny. They are condemned already.

On the day of Pentecost, when Peter preached that the Jews had crucified the One whom God had named as Lord and Christ, "they were pricked in their heart, and said unto Peter and to the rest of the apos-tles, Men and brethren, what shall we do?" (Acts 2:37). During Paul's imprisonment Felix asked Paul to preach to him. And we read that "as he reasoned of righteousness, temperance, and judgment to come, Felix trembled" (24:25). The hearers were convicted of the Spirit. Fortunately many at Pentecost repented; but sadly, Felix merely put off such a commitment. Those who yield to the Spirit's conviction experience the new birth.

None of us can convict sinners or regenerate them; only God's Spirit can do these inward miracles. However, He uses our testimony to do His work of grace when we witness in the power of the Spirit.

A Teacher of Truth (John 16:12-15)

Why were the disciples not yet able to bear all that Jesus wanted to teach them? What was the work of the Spirit of truth as a teacher? How does the Spirit glorify Jesus?

16:12-15: I have yet many things to say unto you, but ye cannot bear them now. [13]Howbeit when he, the Spirit of truth, is come, he will guide you into all truth: for he shall not speak of himself; but whatsoever he shall hear, that shall he speak: and he will show you things to come. [14]He shall glorify me: for he shall receive of mine, and shall show it unto you. [15]All things that the Father hath are mine: therefore said I, that he shall take of mine, and shall show it unto you.

Jesus had taught the disciples many things, but He had still had **many things to say unto** them. Unfortunately, they could not **bear them** at that time. **Bear** translates *bastazein*. This word is used of workers bearing the heat of the day (Matt. 20:12), of believers bearing one another's burdens (Gal. 6:2), and of strong believers bearing with the infirmities of their weak brothers (Rom. 15:1). Jesus used this word on His last night to refer to their unreadiness to hear and understand all He wanted to teach them. We can see this in their failure to understand the necessity of the cross until after the resurrection.

Although the apostles were not yet ready to be taught some things, **the Spirit of truth** would be their Teacher. After Pentecost the Spirit would continue to teach them. He would **guide** them **into all truth.** **Guide** translates *hodegesei*, a verb related to the word *hodos*, or "way." Jesus is the way, the truth, and the life. His Spirit would guide them to understand and follow Him. **All truth** refers to all the truth they needed to serve Him. The Spirit does not speak for Himself, but He speaks and reveals the things of the Father and the Son. **Things to come** refers to all that was future at the time. This includes events of the end times, but it also includes all the development of the way of Christ during the apostolic era.

Two truths need to be kept in mind:

• For one thing, the Spirit does not guide His people into anything that is contradictory to God's revelation in Jesus Christ. The Gospel account of the coming, life, death, and resurrection of Jesus is the objective body of truth with which the Spirit works. He does not lead any of His followers to think or live in some way contrary to what Jesus said and did. Any spirit that is contrary to the way of Jesus is not the

Spirit of truth. No new and different revelation claimed by human beings is true. The Spirit **glorifies** Jesus, not Himself.

• At the same time, the Spirit leads believers into deeper under-standings of the way of Jesus. He also guides believers to see applica-tions of the gospel to contemporary situations. This was true in the days following Pentecost, and it has continued to be true throughout Christian history. When Jesus spoke these words in the upper room, the New Testament had not been written. As the four Gospels were writ-ten, the Spirit reminded the apostles what Jesus said and did. The Spirit also inspired the writers of the Book of Acts, the Epistles, and the Book of Revelation—in other words, the rest of the New Testament.

❖ *Spiritual Transformations*

In "Search the Scriptures" we have seen that the Spirit abides with believers, works in the lives of believers to bear faithful witness to Jesus Christ, convicts the world of its sin, and guides believers into all truth.

Each of these four truths is important in letting these passages impact our lives. The continuing presence of God the Father and Jesus the Son of God are within each believer and among all believers. We can be effective witnesses of Jesus Christ not in our own strength but in the power of the Spirit. He, not human witnesses, convicts lost people of their sins and causes people to be born anew; however, He does work through human witnesses. He continues to guide believers of each generation to see the meaning of Christ for their own time. He inspired the New Testament writers, and He illumines the minds and hearts of believers as they study the Word of God.

*What experiences show you that the Spirit of the Lord abides with you?*_____

How have you experienced or witnessed the convicting work of the Spirit? _____

How does the Spirit give you an increasing understanding of God's Word in your life? _____

*How have you been a Spirit-filled witness for the Lord?*_____

Prayer of Commitment: Lord, may Your Spirit abide with me and help me to witness for You. May I trust Him to convict the lost and to lead me into all Your truth. Amen.

[1]Leon Morris, *The Gospel According to John,* 666.

FULFILLING JESUS' PRAYER

Background Passage: John 17:1-26
Focal Passage: John 17:6-11,15-18,20-26
Key Verses: John 17:20-21

❖ *Significance of the Lesson*

• The *Theme* of this lesson is that Jesus prayed that His followers might have unity with Him, the Father, and one another.

• The *Life Question* this lesson seeks to address is, What does Jesus want for His followers?

• The *Biblical Truth* is that Jesus wants His followers to be unified as a witness for Him to the world.

• The *Life Impact* is to help you work toward unity among Christ's people.

Prayer and Unity

In the secular worldview, self-interest rules the day. "What's in it for me?" "How will this benefit me?" and "What about my rights?" are not merely voiced as questions but are viewed as essential and justifiable demands. It is the age of the individual and "free agent." The good of the group is not an important consideration for many people. Resulting fragmentation and insolation is viewed as the price to be paid for taking care of one's own interests and getting ahead in life.

In the biblical worldview, believers not only have a personal relationship with the Lord but also have a relationship with others who know Him. God desires that believers demonstrate their oneness in Christ before unbelievers. Christ makes possible this unity of spirit. This oneness is a testimony before the world that the gospel is true. Jesus' prayer in John 17 is a powerful encouragement for today's Christians to pray for others and to work toward unity (not uniformity) of God's people.

Jesus and Prayer

The Gospels record many occasions when Jesus prayed. He prayed at His baptism (Luke 3:21), before He called the twelve (6:12), at the transfiguration (9:29), and on many other occasions. Three of His seven sayings on the cross were prayers (23:34,46; Mark 15:34). He prayed at the tomb of Lazarus (John 11:41-42) and in Gethsemane (Matt. 26:42; Mark 14:36; Luke 22:42). However, the longest by far of His recorded prayers is in John 17. This was His great high priestly prayer. Sometimes it is called "The Lord's Prayer," since it is a prayer actually prayed by Jesus. John's Gospel does not record the prayer of Jesus in the garden of Gethsemane on His last night; instead, it records this great prayer in John 17. However, John 17:1-5—like the prayer recorded in the Synoptic Gospels—was also a prayer for Jesus to be able to finish His redemptive mission. In John 12:21-33, the finishing of His mission was at hand. He would be glorified by being lifted up on the cross. The purpose of His glorification was that people should come to know eternal life. This is the meaning of Jesus' prayer: "Father, the hour is come; glorify thy Son, that thy Son also may glorify thee" (17:1).

In John 17 Jesus prayed for Himself (vv. 1-5), for the apostles (vv. 6-19), and for future believers (vv. 20-26).

Word Study: *Pray*

Several Greek words are translated *pray* in the New Testament. However, *erotao* is the only one found in the Gospel of John. It also means "to ask" and is used of asking something of another person (16:5,23,30). This is the word John used for the prayers of Jesus (14:16; 16:26; 17:9,15,20).

❖ *Search the Scriptures*

On the night before His crucifixion, Jesus prayed that the Father would keep the apostles so that they would have the kind of oneness the Father and Son had. He asked the Father to help them be in but not of the world so that they could be sent forth to fulfill the mission entrusted to them. Jesus also prayed for future generations so that they might have the kind of oneness that would be a positive testimony for the world.

Prayer for His Disciples (John 17:6-11)

What verbs are used in verses 6-8 for the actions of the Father, the Son, and the apostles? Did Jesus ever pray for the world? For what did He ask for the apostles?

Verses 6-8: I have manifested thy name unto the men which thou gavest me out of the world: thine they were, and thou gavest them me; and they have kept thy word. ⁷Now they have known that all things whatsoever thou hast given me are of thee. ⁸For I have given unto them the words which thou gavest me; and they have received them, and have known surely that I came out from thee, and they have believed that thou didst send me.

For whom was Jesus praying in these verses? Verse 12 makes clear that He had in mind the apostles minus Judas. Verse 20 also makes clear that Jesus began by praying for the apostles.

These verses summarize the actions of God the Father, Jesus the Son, and the apostles. Look at the verses and identify which verbs apply to each. The Father **sent** Jesus into the world. He also gave **(gavest)** the apostles to Jesus. God gave Jesus the **words** for Him to give to the apostles. Jesus **manifested** ("revealed," NIV) God's **name** to them. Jesus gave them the words God had given to Him for them.

Some key words appear to describe the apostles' responses to the actions of the Father and Son. They **kept** ("obeyed," NIV) God's **word.** They knew that **all things whatsoever** the Father had given the Son were from God. They **received** them. Jesus said, **They have believed that thou didst send me.** Notice the key emphases: *obeyed, knew, received,* and *believed.* These responses are true of all believers, but they were first true of the apostles.

Verses 9-11: I pray for them: I pray not for the world, but for them which thou hast given me; for they are thine. ¹⁰And all mine are thine, and thine are mine; and I am glorified in them. ¹¹And now I am no more in the world, but these are in the world, and I come to thee. Holy Father, keep through thine own name those whom thou hast given me, that they may be one, as we are.

Jesus emphasized that this prayer was for His followers, **not for the world.** This does not mean that He had no concern for the lost, sinful world. John 3:16 emphasizes God's love for the world. Later in this prayer Jesus spoke of the holiness of His people, which is inseparable from their mission to the lost world (vv. 15-19). The purpose of that mission was that the sinful people of the world might believe and be saved (v. 18). He prayed for the oneness of His followers, one purpose of which was that unbelievers might believe (vv. 21,23).

Thus Jesus' prayer showed no lack of concern for the unbelieving world, but He prayed for His followers who were the ones who must bear His message to that lost world. If they were not all they should be, the lost world might never hear the good news.

Of the apostles, Jesus said to the Father, **They are thine.** He added, **All mine are thine, and thine are mine.** Jesus said that He was **glorified in them.** In the Bible, to be **glorified** meant that God had His full nature made known. To put it another way, it was to have His reputation equal to His character.

Verse 11 shows what Jesus asked for God to do for the apostles. Jesus Himself was about to leave the **world.** The apostles continued to live **in the world.** Later He would pray that they not be **of the world** (vv. 14,16). Jesus addressed God as **Holy Father.** He requested God to **keep** them **through** the Father's **own name.** He was to keep them, Jesus prayed, **that they may be one, as we are.**

Jesus knew that the apostles would face many trials and temptations. He also knew that only God's grace and power could protect and preserve them faithful. Thus He prayed this for them. He was ultimately concerned for their oneness of spirit as they served the Lord. These apostles were different individuals. They easily could have allowed dissension to keep them from fulfilling the mission God had for them. Unity was essential for the successful completion of their mission.

Prayer for His Disciples' Mission (John 17:15-18)

*What happens when God's people are **in the world** and **of the world**? Why is withdrawing from the world not the answer? How can believers be in but not of the world? Since Christ defeated Satan, why is he still a threat? What is the relationship between holy living and fulfilling Christ's mission? What happens when believers try to have one without the other?*

Verses 15-18: **I pray not that thou shouldest take them out of the world, but that thou shouldest keep them from the evil.** [16]**They are not of the world, even as I am not of the world.** [17]**Sanctify them through thy truth: thy word is truth.** [18]**As thou hast sent me into the world, even so have I also sent them into the world.**

In verse 16, Jesus said of the apostles, **they are not of the world, even as I am not of the world.** He repeated this emphasis from verse 14. This truth is the key to verses 15-17. Jesus was about to leave the earth, but even while He was here He was not really of the world. **World** is used in verses 15-16 to refer not to the physical creation of this earth but to refer to the sinful way of living of the people of this world. Jesus came to save this lost world (3:16). He interacted with the sinful people of the world. He was known as a friend of sinners. However, He did not partake of the sins of the people whom He befriended.

Jesus wanted His apostles to follow His example. For them to do this required that they be *in* but not *of* the world. Over the centuries believers have tended to err in one of two directions. All too often they have been in the world and of the world at the same time. Leonard Griffith wrote, "The Church has become so identified with the world's way of thinking and so enslaved to the world's standard of values that it stands in danger of losing that which makes it a Church, a community of Christians who by their godlike character are separate and distinct from the world in which they live."[1]

Do you think he overstated this, or is he correct in his analysis? Do our churches stand over against the world's way and values, or do the churches often reflect the ways of the world? The same question, of course, needs to be asked of each of us who professes to follow Christ.

The evil translates *tou ponerou*. The same combination is found in the Model Prayer (Matt. 6:13). Since the article is used, most modern versions prefer to translate it "the evil one" (NIV, HCSB, NKJV, NASB, NRSV, REB, CEV). Jesus knew that the apostles and those who followed them would be tempted by the Evil One to compromise with the world. Thus Jesus did not ask the Father to take His people out of the world but to **keep them from the evil** one. Jesus knew that His death and resurrection would inflict a mortal wound on the prince of this world (12:31), but He also knew that Satan would devote himself to carry with him to destruction as many as possible. Thus Jesus prayed that the Father would protect them from the clutches of Satan. He knew that God could not keep them from having any contact with the devil; therefore, He prayed that God would protect them from the Evil One's power (Jas. 4:7; 1 Pet. 5:8).

Jesus had told Peter: "Simon, Simon, Satan has asked to sift you as wheat. But I have prayed for you, Simon, that your faith may not fail. And when you have turned back, strengthen your brothers"

(Luke 22:31-32, NIV). Jesus prayed a similar prayer for all the apostles in John 17:15. Hebrews 7:25 tells us that He now prays for all His followers. What a reassurance that is!

Some Christians seek to withdraw from this evil world to some sanctuary where they will not be tempted by the sinful world. Notice that this was not what Jesus wanted: **I pray not that thou shouldest take them out of the world.** He knew, of course, that no one of us sinful creatures can find on earth any sanctuary where we will not be tempted. The history of monastic living confirms this. Even if we could, how could we then fulfill our calling to represent Christ in the world?

In the petition **Sanctify them through thy truth,** the word **sanctify** translates *hagiason,* from which we get our words for holy living. The word means "to set apart." Those whom God sets apart He sets apart for holy living and for dedicated service. These two go together. Verse 17 emphasizes the holy living. Verse 18 stresses the mission. Jesus said that He had **sent** the apostles **into the world** in the same way that the Father had **sent** Him **into the world.** After His resurrection, Jesus told the apostles, "As my Father hath sent me, even so send I you" (20:21).

As Christians, we must avoid the opposite dangers of moral compromise and self-righteous exclusivism. As Christians, we must maintain the balance between holy living and faithful and loving witness for the Lord to an unbelieving world. Failure to live in God's way will undercut any effective witness to sinners. Failure to go on mission into the world will fail to take the good news to them. "*When the Church loses its sense of mission, it loses its reason for being. . . .* Too often the Church resembles a coastguard station on a dangerous coast where the successors of the founders come together simply to hear stories of the rescue service but where the actual launching out into the ocean storm has become a hireling vocation or one left to a few volunteers."[2]

Only Jesus perfectly balanced holiness and love, but He prayed for God to help His followers to do the same.

Prayer for Future Disciples (John 17:20-26)

Are these the only verses in the prayer that apply to future believers? How does verse 20 show Jesus' confidence in the success of the gospel mission? What expressions of oneness can believers today demonstrate? What is the purpose of such oneness? Does verse 24 refer to this life or to heaven?

Verses 20-23: **Neither pray I for these alone, but for them also which shall believe on me through their word; [21]that they all may be one; as thou, Father, art in me, and I in thee, that they also may be one in us: that the world may believe that thou hast sent me. [22]And the glory which thou gavest me I have given them; that they may be one, even as we are one: [23]I in them, and thou in me, that they may be made perfect in one; and that the world may know that thou hast sent me, and hast loved them, as thou hast loved me.**

Jesus prayed not only for the apostles who had some unique aspects to their mission (they were eyewitnesses), He also prayed for those who **shall believe on me through their word.** This referred to other believers in the first century, and it refers to believers of all ages. We too have believed the witness of the apostles, which is now in written form in the New Testament. Verse 20 shows Jesus' confidence in the ultimate success of the good news. He was about to die, and things looked bleak for any future for Him and His cause; however, Jesus trusted God to raise Him from the dead, to send the Holy Spirit, to lead the apostles to bear faithful testimony, and to convict and convert lost people. He expected this to continue until His future coming.

The theme of verses 21-23 is oneness. This is the fourth main petition the Lord prayed for His followers. The other three were for security (v. 11), holiness (vv. 15-17), and faithfulness in mission (v. 18). Jesus already had prayed that God would protect the apostles that they might be one as He and the Father were one (v. 11). Now He prayed for future believers, asking that **they all may be one; as thou, Father, art in me, and I in thee.** The oneness of believers was to be like the oneness of the Father and the Son. They were to **be one in us.** One purpose of this oneness would be **that the world may believe.** Jesus said that He had given believers His **glory** in order **that they may be one** in the Father and the Son even as they **are one.** He also prayed that future believers would **be made perfect in one** ("brought to complete unity," NIV; "perfected in unity," NASB).

The meaning and application of this oneness has been debated over the centuries and has itself become a source of dissension. Throughout history there have been groups who insisted that the only way to have oneness is to have all believers belong to the same earthly organization. This was the view of the official state church that led to internal corruption and the inquisition. Wherever there has been one established church with government sponsorship and support, the results have not glorified the Lord. Baptists have always insisted on religious freedom for all believers. In the United States religion has flourished in this atmosphere of freedom.

Having said this, however, strife and war among Christians has been a sorry testimony to the world. Baptists and others have insisted that salvation is by grace through faith in Christ. This is not a matter of denominational affiliation but of personal relationship with the Lord. Thus although we cannot agree with all the beliefs of other Christians, we can affirm our oneness in Christ with others who believe Jesus is the only way to God, the truth, and the life (14:6).

Of course, it goes without saying that in a local congregation, oneness of spirit is crucial for winning people to the Lord.

Verses 24-26: **Father, I will that they also, whom thou hast given me, be with me where I am; that they may behold my glory, which thou hast given me: for thou lovedst me before the foundation of the world. ²⁵O righteous Father, the world hath not known thee: but I have known thee, and these have known that thou hast sent me. ²⁶And I have declared unto them thy name, and will declare it: that the love wherewith thou hast loved me may be in them, and I in them.**

Verse 24 probably spells out how oneness of believers will be perfected. Most Bible students believe that Jesus was speaking in this verse of the future perfection of believers in the coming new heavens and new earth. Jesus prayed that those whom God would give Him would **be with me where I am.** Jesus said that He was going to prepare a place for them and then come and bring them to be with Him (14:2-3). At that time, believers will **behold** His **glory,** which God gave Him **before the foundation of the world.** Heaven will be the perfect expression of every aspect of the Christian life: faith and fellowship with the Lord, moral likeness to Jesus, and perfect fellowship with others. The idea that heaven will have separate places for different groups of believers is not a biblical teaching. The biblical pictures of the future life show all believers together praising the same Lord.

Verses 25-26 reinforce the entire prayer by repeating some of its key emphases, Remember, this was a prayer to the **righteous Father.** Only He can make that which has been asked for a reality, but He expects us to do our part in being what He wants us to be. And under it all stands the foundation of the amazing **love** of the Father for humanity.

❖ *Spiritual Transformations*

In "Search the Scriptures" we have seen Jesus' prayer for the apostles. He asked the Lord to protect them, to sanctify them, and to fulfill His mission. In praying for future generations of believers Jesus emphasized the need for oneness.

How do you feel when someone says, "I'm praying for you"? This should encourage us. How much more encouraging to know that Jesus prayed for us and in heaven still prays for us! John 17 shows us what He asks God to do for us.

Focus on the four basic petitions of this prayer, for they apply to believers today.

Security: Jesus prayed that the Lord would guard, keep, or protect believers from the power and clutches of the Evil One. For our part, this calls on us to entrust ourselves into His care and keeping and to rely on His strength to overcome temptations.

Holiness: The Lord wants us to live in the way that God has set us apart to live. Jesus prayed that believers might be *in* but not *of* the world.

Mission: We are called to live holy lives in order to have a basis for bold witnessing to unbelievers. He sends us into the world as the Father sent Him into the world.

Oneness: In every way possible, Jesus wants believers to express the oneness that all true believers have in Jesus Christ. Such unity is a gift from God, but one in which we are expected to do our part.

In what ways has the Lord's protecting hand been on you? _____
_____
How well are you living in *but not* of *the world?* _____
*How are you on mission for the Lord to an unbelieving world?*_____
_____
In what ways do you express your oneness in Christ with other believers? _____

Prayer of Commitment: Lord, protect us, set us apart to live for You, empower us for mission, and help us express our oneness in You. Amen.

[1]Leonard Griffith, *The Eternal Legacy from an Upper Room*, 160.
[2]Griffith, *The Eternal Legacy from an Upper Room*, 168.

ANTICIPATING RESURRECTION

Background Passage: 1 Corinthians 15:1-26
Focal Passage: 1 Corinthians 15:3-8,12-20
Key Verse: 1 Corinthians 15:20

❖ *Significance of the Lesson*

• The *Theme* of this lesson is that Jesus' resurrection guarantees that believers are made alive, have victory over death, and will experience the resurrection.

• The *Life Question* addressed by this lesson is, What does Jesus' resurrection mean to me?

• The *Biblical Truth* is that because Christ arose from the dead, believers also will experience resurrection.

• The *Life Impact* is to help you live each day in anticipation of the resurrection.

• This is the annual *Easter Coordinated Evangelism Lesson.*

Life, Death, and Resurrection

In the secular worldview, this life is all that people have. Thus people try to get as much out of this life as they can, any way they can. Life often is lived from a selfish perspective and motivation. Because secular-minded people have no real hope of life beyond death, they feel a sense of despair. They often try to drown out their despair by acts of selfish indulgence. Some secular people have a vague hope of some kind of existence beyond this life, but it is not the eternal life depicted in the Bible.

In the biblical worldview, the resurrection of Jesus Christ from the dead provides for believers confident hope of deliverance from spiritual death in this life, of going to be with the Lord at death, and of participation in the future resurrection at the consummation of all things. Thus Christians need not deny death; instead, they can defy death.

The Corinthians and the Resurrection

First Corinthians contains Paul's answers to many questions and problems that were troubling the church at Corinth. The final problem dealt with in Paul's letter concerned death and resurrection. Clues to the nature of the problem are found in what Paul wrote in 15:12 and in the way he dealt with the issue in the chapter as a whole. Since the church was in a cosmopolitan center with many diverse philosophies of life, the problem may have involved more than one factor. One possibility is that many did not believe in any kind of life after death. This was true of many first-century people, and it is true of many today. The second possibility is that some of them believed that the resurrection of believers had already taken place (2 Tim. 2:17-18). There is some truth in this, for believers already have experienced passing from spiritual death to spiritual life (John 5:24; Rom. 6:3-4). Apparently these people denied any future resurrection. The third possibility is that 1 Corinthians 15:12 refers to Greek believers who believed in the immortality of the soul but not in the resurrection of the body. The idea of a resurrected body was contrary to most Greek philosophies (Acts 17:32). How Paul dealt with the problem in 1 Corinthians 15:21-57 makes this third view the most likely.

Word Study: *Firstfruits*

The Greek word for *firstfruits* in verse 20 is *aparche*. Its literal reference was to the first part of the harvest. This was to be offered to the Lord before any of the rest was used for personal needs or for sale. Romans 11:16 is an example of its literal meaning. In the New Testament the word is more often used figuratively. It refers to the first converts in a given region (Rom. 16:5), to Christians as a kind of firstfruits of all God's creatures (Jas. 1:18), to the firstfruits of the Spirit (Rom. 8:23), and to the resurrection of Jesus as the firstfruits of the dead in Christ (1 Cor. 15:23). Because of His resurrection as the first of the harvest, believers also will be raised.

❖ *Search the Scriptures*

The heart of the gospel is the death of Jesus for our sins and His resurrection from the dead. The evidence of the reality of His resurrection was His appearances to so many individuals and groups. If Christians will not be raised, then Christ has not been raised; and if that were true, all that Christians believe and hope is false. But Christ has been raised; therefore, believers also will be raised.

The Reality of Christ's Resurrection (1 Cor. 15:3-8)

Why do we believe that the cross and the resurrection are the basic content of the saving gospel? Name the individuals and groups to whom the risen Lord appeared. Why did Paul include himself in this list? How are these appearances evidence for the reality of Christ's resurrection?

Verse 3-4: For I delivered unto you first of all that which I also received, how that Christ died for our sins according to the scriptures; ⁴and that he was buried, and that he rose again the third day according to the scriptures.

Paul began this final section of his letter by reminding the Corinthian Christians of the good news that he had preached, that they had believed, and by which they were saved (vv. 1-2). Then he summarized the content of the good news of salvation. He focused on the death and resurrection of Jesus. Paul did not make up these events. The words **delivered** and **received** were used of the Christian message, which was told by believers to unbelievers. **Delivered** translates *paredoka,* which means "to hand over" or "pass along." It was used of what Judas did in handing over or betraying Christ, and it was used of believers passing along to others the content of the good news or the teachings of Jesus (see Luke 1:2; 1 Cor. 11:23). **First of all** refers to that which was "of first importance" (NIV).

The words **Christ died for our sins according to the scriptures** include three affirmations: First, **Christ died.** He was unjustly condemned and crucified. At that time, His enemies thought they had won a victory; His followers thought they had sustained a terrible defeat. Jesus' resurrection, however, led them to rethink the cross. Second, they came to realize that Jesus died **for our sins.** Jesus' death was atonement for the sins of the world: "God was in Christ, reconciling the world unto himself" (2 Cor. 5:19); "He hath made him to be sin for us, who knew no sin; that we might be made the righteousness of God in him" (v. 21); "When we were yet without strength, in due time Christ died for the ungodly" (Rom. 5:6). Third, they recognized that His atoning death was **according to the scriptures.** After the resurrection, the risen Lord taught them concerning the Old Testament passages He had fulfilled (Luke 24:44-45). They saw that passages such as Isaiah 53 had their ultimate fulfillment in Jesus' suffering and death.

third ~~Second~~, **he was buried.** All four Gospels tell how Jesus' body was placed in a tomb made available by Joseph of Arimathea. The mention of His burial reinforces the fact that Jesus was truly dead.

Fourth ~~Third~~, **he rose again the third day according to the scriptures.** **Rose again,** *egegertai,* is perfect passive. This shows that Jesus "was raised" (NIV) by God. It can be translated "has been raised." The two earlier verbs for **died** and **was buried** are in the aorist tense, which refers to an action at some point. The perfect tense refers to an act in the past that continues in the present. "Christ died, but he is not dead; he was buried, but he is not in the grave; he was raised, and he is alive now."[1] **The third day** includes the time from Friday afternoon until Sunday morning (Luke 23:54–24:1). The resurrection of Jesus was foretold in **scriptures** such as Isaiah 53:10-12. *notes*

Verses 5-8: And that he was seen of Cephas, then of the twelve: After that, he was seen of above five hundred brethren at once; of whom the greater part remain unto this present, but some are fallen asleep. [7]After that, he was seen of James; then of all the apostles. [8]And last of all he was seen of me also, as of one born out of due time.

Paul then listed six of the appearances of the risen Lord. The word *ophthe* (**was seen**; "appeared," NIV) is used four times. **Cephas** was the Aramaic word for "stone," the nickname Jesus gave to Simon Peter (John 1:42). The Corinthians knew Cephas well. He was one of the leaders over whom they argued (1 Cor. 1:12). This appearance to Simon Peter is also mentioned as happening on the day of Jesus' resurrection (Luke 24:34). Neither Paul nor Luke described what happened at this meeting of the risen Lord and the disciple who had denied Him three times. John 21:15-22 records a later appearance to Peter.

Jesus also appeared to **the twelve.** Actually, since Judas was dead, there were only eleven; but this expression had become a somewhat technical term for the ones who had been with Him. These appearances are mentioned in Matthew 28:16-17; Luke 24:33-51; and John 20:19-29. Keep in mind that none of the apostles was expecting Jesus to be raised from the dead. Although Jesus had predicted His death and His resurrection, they never truly heard what He said about the resurrection because they were hung up on His prediction of suffering and death. Thus the disciples had to be fully convinced that they saw the Lord alive. They did not merely see a vision of a spirit; they saw the Lord in His glorified body.

Only Paul mentioned Jesus' appearance to **above five hundred brethren.** We are not sure which of the appearances Paul had in mind. Perhaps it was one not recorded in the Gospels, or it may have been the appearance when He gave the Great Commission (Matt. 28:18-20) or just before His ascension (Acts 1:9). Paul emphasized that most of these people were still alive when he wrote the Corinthians over 20 years later. In other words, these witnesses could confirm that Jesus is alive.

Paul is also the only one to mention the appearance to **James.** The half brother of Jesus did not believe in Jesus during His ministry (John 7:5), but he was among the 120 who prayed before Pentecost (Acts 1:14). Jesus' appearance to James may have made the difference.

Paul also reported an appearance **to all the apostles.** Paul already had mentioned the ones whom we generally call "the apostles," but at times the word is used of a larger group of missionaries whom Jesus had sent out.

The apostle Paul included himself among those who had seen the risen Lord. He believed His experience on the Damascus road was more than a vision of spiritual things. He believed the risen Lord made this special revelation to him. Paul recognized that he was not one of the twelve and that the appearance to him came after the ascension. He, therefore, referred to himself as **one born out of due time.** In Greek, **born out of due time** is one word, *ektromati*. Translators search for the best English words to translate *ektromati*: "abnormally born" (NIV, HCSB), "untimely born," (NASB, NRSV), "born at the wrong time" (CEV). Paul admitted that the appearance to him was unique in time and manner, but he insisted that the risen Lord appeared to him and commissioned him to be an apostle.

What was Paul's purpose in listing these appearances? He was showing the evidence for the reality of Christ's resurrection from the dead. Skeptics must deal with this evidence. They must come up with a better explanation for the objective phenomena concerning the resurrection. The objective phenomena are these: (1) The disciples claimed to have seen the risen Lord. (2) Their lives were changed, and by this message the lives of others were changed. (3) For 20 centuries changes in individuals and society have been attributed to the living Lord. Skeptics simply respond by saying that no one could have been raised from the dead because dead people do not come back to life. This prejudiced statement fails to consider the evidence.

Suppose someone said: "I don't believe that Alexander the Great conquered the world in his day. How could a young king of a second-rate country defeat the mighty Persian Empire and win so many battles when his forces were outnumbered and often far from their home base? There may have been a king of Macedonia called Alexander, but I can't believe he did all the things for which he is given credit."

How would you answer such a skeptic? You could point to the writings of historians, some of whom were with Alexander. You could point to a city in Egypt bearing his name. You could point to the fact that something spread the Greek language and culture over the civilized world. All of these are strong evidences of Alexander and his conquests.

The objective evidences for the resurrection of Jesus are even more impressive. There are the testimonies of a wide number and variety of people who saw Him alive after His death. The early believers surely believed that He was raised from the dead. There is the evidence of His influence in history—longer, more profound, and more helpful than the influence of Alexander or any other person. The reality of Christ's resurrection is not to be doubted.

The Hopelessness of No Resurrection (1 Cor. 15:12-18)

What was the problem in Corinth concerning the resurrection of the dead? How did Paul show the relation of Christ's resurrection and Christians' resurrection? What would be different if Christ was not raised from the dead? What three words did Paul use to show what life would be like if Christ was not raised from the dead?

Verses 12-13: Now if Christ be preached that he rose from the dead, how say some among you that there is no resurrection of the dead? [13]But if there be no resurrection of the dead, then is Christ not risen.

What Paul wrote strongly implies that the Corinthians were not denying Christ's resurrection but a future resurrection of believers in Christ. Some of them were saying, **There is no resurrection of the dead.** This might include Christ's resurrection, but it probably referred to the future resurrection of believers.

In verse 13 Paul wrote, **If there be no resurrection of the dead, then is Christ not risen.** Although Paul had used verses 5-11 to demonstrate the certainty of Jesus' resurrection, the Corinthians seemed not to have doubted that. Instead, they denied that believers would experience a future resurrection. In verses 14-18 Paul showed the terrible results of denying either resurrection. Denying the resurrection of Christians denies the resurrection of Jesus. And if He was not raised, all is lost.

Verses 14-18: **And if Christ be not risen, then is our preaching vain, and your faith is also vain. ¹⁵Yea, and we are found false witnesses of God; because we have testified of God that he raised up Christ: whom he raised not up, if so be that the dead rise not. ¹⁶For if the dead rise not, then is not Christ raised: ¹⁷and if Christ be not raised, your faith is vain; ye are yet in your sins. ¹⁸Then they also which are fallen asleep in Christ are perished.**

These powerful verses give us a vision of the dark world if Jesus had not been raised from the dead. Paul mentioned several areas of Christianity that would be totally changed: **preaching, faith,** testimony, salvation, hope of life after death. He used three words to show the negative results **if Christ be not risen.**

One word is **vain** (*kenos*). Paul used this word of **preaching** and **faith.** Paul said that if Christ was not raised from the dead, Christian preaching is vain. This word for **vain** means "without reality," "empty" (NKJV), or "useless" (NIV). Paul said the same thing about their **faith.** In other words, without a resurrection their trust in the living God is empty and without reality ("null and void," REB, NEB).

Paul used another word for **vain** in describing **faith** in verse 17, *mataia.* Although at times these words were used interchangeably, here they seem to have retained their distinctive meanings. *Mataia* means "without effect" or "futile" (NIV, NRSV). Paul gave an example of the ineffectiveness of such faith when he stated, **Ye are yet in your sins.** They may have thought that their faith had saved them from their sins; but if Christ was not raised from the dead, they were still lost in sin. Then Paul added that without the resurrection the dead in Christ have **perished.**

The third word is *pseudo,* which is found in the compound word for **false witnesses** (*pseudomartures*). In other words, Christian beliefs and actions are empty, futile, and false if Christ has not been raised from the dead.

Think of all the **preaching** you have heard—in your church and elsewhere. All of it is without reality and false if Christ is not alive. Think about your **faith**—your beliefs and your trust in God. It is without reality if Christ is not alive. Recall all the testimonies you have given and heard. All are false if Christ is not alive. Think about your salvation and new life. If Christ was not raised from the dead, you **are yet in your sins.** The good news being without any real effect left you as you were before you repented and believed. Think of the times when you have been at the grave of loved ones in Christ and hoped to be reunited with them in the new heavens and new earth. If Christ has not been raised from the dead, there is no victory over death. If Christ is not alive, the dead in Christ are not with the Lord awaiting the resurrection; they have died and that was the end of them.

Throughout this passage Paul insisted that Christ's resurrection and believers' resurrection are inseparable. You can't have one without the other. Verse 16 repeats this theme from verse 13: **If the dead rise not, then is not Christ raised.**

If Christ was not raised from the dead, redemptive history ended in a grave. "Then God is not the living God, nor is he the God of the living as Jesus said (Mk. 12:27). Death is stronger than God; death is stronger than God's word. God's acts are proven futile in the face of man's greatest enemy—death."[2]

The resurrection of Jesus is the foundation for all that Christians believe, do, and hope. If this foundation is removed, all else crumbles.

A favorite movie at Christmas time is *It's a Wonderful Life.* It is the story of a small-town man named George Bailey, who in a time of despair believes everyone would be better off if he never had been born. He is led to see the many differences for good that his life had made. How much greater is the eternal good that results from the resurrection of Jesus Christ? Just contemplating how life would be changed without Him is devastating.

The Assurance of Believers' Resurrection (1 Cor. 15:19-20)

When are believers most pitiable? How did Paul proclaim the truth of the resurrection of Christ and of believers? In what sense are the dead sleeping? When do believers go to be with the Lord? What makes the difference between denying death and defying death?

Verse 19: **If in this life only we have hope in Christ, we are of all men most miserable.**

It is not clear how this verse should be translated. The word translated **only** can go with **in this life** or it can go with **hope.** Most translations assume that it goes with **in this life**: "If only for this life we have hope in Christ, we are to be pitied more than all men" (NIV). If this is correct, the focus is on the importance of life beyond this life. If there is no future resurrection, we are to be pitied for living our lives as if there were. Then the pleasure seekers may be right. "If the dead rise not . . . let us eat and drink; for tomorrow we die" (v. 32).

If **only** goes with **hope,** it would be translated, "If we have only hope in Christ, we are of all men most to be pitied." The point here would be that if our hope is nothing more than the world's empty hopes, without any basis in the God of hope, then such hopes are only wishful thinking. Since both translations represent biblical truths, both options are possible.

***Verse 20:* But now is Christ risen from the dead, and become the firstfruits of them that slept.**

Here is the verse in which Paul brought his first readers back to reality. Notice the beginning **but now.** Paul had not been describing what was real but what would be true if Christ had not been raised from the dead. He described the nightmare conditions if that were true. Now he reminded them that none of those things in verses 14-19 were true because Christ has been raised from the dead: **But now is Christ risen from the dead.** Because He conquered death, He became **the firstfruits of them that slept.** In the "Word Study" we saw that **firstfruits** referred to the first of a harvest. Thus when Jesus was raised from the dead, He became the first of many who would follow Him in resurrection.

The New Testament often refers to the dead in Christ as sleeping. This analogy is found in verses 6,18, and 20. The same description was used in Greek, Roman, and Jewish society. It means that the dead person looks like someone who is asleep. For believers, it also implies that, as in human sleep, the dead will awaken. Jesus used the analogy this way of Jairus's daughter (Matt. 9:24; Luke 8:52) and Lazarus (John 11:11-14).

Paul used the analogy the same way. He used it in this chapter and in 1 Thessalonians 4:13-15 to stress the future resurrection. Some people take the analogy literally and claim that the sleep of death lasts until the resurrection. This view that the dead will rest in a state of unconsciousness until the resurrection is called "soul-sleep." We might draw such a conclusion if we had only the passages in 1 Corinthians 15 and 1 Thessalonians 4; however, we also have Jesus' promise to the dying thief on the cross (Luke 23:43), and we have the statement of Paul, who was looking forward to his death so he could depart to be with the Lord (Phil. 1:23).

When do believers go to be with the Lord? The twofold answer seems to be that each believer's spirit goes to be with the Lord at death, but that the dead in Christ—like the living—look forward to the end of time when they will receive bodies fit for their lives in the new heavens and new earth. Paul answered questions about the nature of this resurrection and the resurrection bodies in the rest of chapter 15. He emphasized that the future resurrection would mean the final victory over death. He denied that the body would be flesh and blood, but he insisted it was a body, which he called a spiritual body. Praising God for His victory over death is more important than being able to understand unanswered questions about the exact nature of heaven and the resurrection body. Paul concluded his statements with the exclamation: "O death, where is thy sting? O grave, where is thy victory? The sting of death is sin; and the strength of sin is the law. But thanks be to God, which giveth us the victory through our Lord Jesus Christ" (vv. 55-57).

❖ *Spiritual Transformations*

In "Search the Scriptures," we have seen how Paul defined the gospel and demonstrated the reality of Jesus' resurrection by listing appearances of the risen Lord. He also insisted that Christ's resurrection would result in the resurrection of believers. Paul did this by showing what would not be true if Christ were not raised from the dead. Christ's resurrection is the foundation for all we believe and hope. Because Christ was raised from the dead, He will deliver His people from death by raising them from the dead.

The "Life Impact" is to help you live each day in anticipation of the resurrection.

Why do you believe in the resurrection of Christ? _____

Why do you believe in believers' resurrection? _____

What difference does—or should—this hope make in your life? __

_____

Prayer of Commitment: Lord, we praise You for Your victory over sin and death. Help us to live in light of that faith and hope. Amen.

[1]C. K. Barrett, *A Commentary on the First Epistle to the Corinthians,* in Harper's New Testament Commentaries [New York: Harper & Row, Publishers, 1968], 340.

[2]George Eldon Ladd, *I Believe in the Resurrection of Jesus* [Grand Rapids: William B. Eerdmans Publishing Company, 1975], 144.

Amos: Prophet to the Nations

Calvin Coolidge was a man of few words. One Sunday after attending church, he was asked what the pastor preached about. Coolidge replied, "Sin." The questioner inquired further, "What did he say about it?" Coolidge said, "He said he was against it."[1]

The Bible is against sin. This is nowhere more apparent than in the Prophets. From Elijah to John the Baptist, all the prophets condemned sin. None condemned it more strongly than Amos. Recently, a fellow church member asked me to recommend a book that would deal with the sins in our society. I suggested that he begin with the Book of Amos. The sins condemned by Amos are the sins of today's world also. This is a four-session study of some key passages in the Book of Amos. Amos was one of four great eighth-century prophets. He and Hosea preached in northern Israel. Isaiah and Micah preached in Judah.

After getting the people's attention by condemning the sin of inhumanity in surrounding nations and briefly mentioning the sins of Judah, Amos focused on the sins of northern Israel. These two nations were God's chosen people with higher accountability for their sins. Amos spoke plainly about Israel's sins. See if any of these sound familiar. Many people's goal was to have enough wealth to have fine homes. The poor were either ignored or exploited. Sexual immorality was condoned and encouraged. Religion was popular, but it was a substitute for the real thing.

The second lesson deals with Israel's sins of injustice and calls on the people to seek the Lord that they might live. Amos also called on them to let justice and righteousness flow like mighty streams. The third lesson tells of a confrontation between Amos and Amaziah the priest of Bethel. Amaziah told Amos to leave the country. Amos withstood these attacks and condemned Amaziah. The final lesson looks beyond the coming judgment on Israel to the hope of God's restoration of His people.

[1]Gorton Carruth and Eugene Ehrlich, *American Quotations* [New York: Wings Books, 1988], 509.

WARNINGS OF DISASTER

Background Passage: Amos 1:1–3:15
Focal Passage: Amos 1:1-5; 2:4-8; 3:7,13-15
Key Verse: Amos 3:7

❖ *Significance of the Lesson*

• The *Theme* of this lesson is that God's judgment extends to all nations of the world.
• The *Life Question* addressed in this lesson is, Does God still judge people and nations today?
• The *Biblical Truth* is that God will judge every individual and nation for specific sins.
• The *Life Impact* is to help you prepare to face God's judgment.

Worldviews About God's Judgment

In the secular worldview, the idea of God's judgment is usually rejected. God is perceived as a doting grandfatherly figure who is permissive about human behavior. The concept of divine judgment for specific sins is foreign to this worldview.

The biblical worldview is that God is sovereign over His universe. He holds nations and individuals accountable for being true to His revealed standards. Those nations and individuals who transgress those standards will be judged unless they repent.

Word Study: *Visit*

The word **visit,** which is used twice in 3:14, translates the Hebrew word *paqad*. This primitive root meant "to attend to," "to visit," "to muster," or "to report." However, when the Lord visited the people in judgment, the word took on the idea of punishment. Thus most modern translations render it "punish" at least once in 3:14 (NKJV [1], NIV [1], CEV [1], NASB [2], NRSV [2]).

❖ *Search the Scriptures*

Amos described the Lord as a roaring lion. He condemned the sins of Syria, the nations surrounding Israel, Judah, and Israel. He predicted sure judgment on unfaithful Israel.

Proximity of Judgment (Amos 1:1-2)

What was Amos's vocation? Where was he from? Where did he preach? When did he do his work in preaching? What was Israel like in that time? What was his basic message?

1:1: The words of Amos, who was among the herdmen of Tekoa, which he saw concerning Israel in the days of Uzziah king of Judah, and in the days of Jeroboam the son of Joash king of Israel, two years before the earthquake.

Verse 1 introduces **the words of Amos.** However, repeatedly in his messages Amos claimed to be delivering "the words of the Lord" (1:3, REB, NEB). Amos spoke the words, but he spoke in the name of God.

Amos was **among the herdmen** ("one of the shepherds," NIV) by vocation. This description is amplified in 7:14, where Amos called himself "an herdman, and a gatherer of sycamore fruit" ("I also took care of sycamore-fig trees," NIV). The usual word for **shepherds** is in verse 2. The word in verse 1 is *noqed.* "*Noqed* is not the word for 'shepherd' but designates Amos as a breeder/tender of livestock (sheep and goats; cf. 'sheep-breeder,' REB). This assessment is based on 2 Kgs. 3:4, the only other text in the Old Testament where the term is used."[1] The wide variety of translations for the word in verse 1 shows the possibilities ("among the sheepbreeders," NKJV; "one of the sheep-farmers," REB, NEB). Another word, *boqer*, in 7:14 refers to a "herdsman" (NASB).

Amos was from **Tekoa** [tih-KOH-uh], a town in the Southern Kingdom of Judah, about 10 miles south of Jerusalem. He did his preaching in **Israel,** the Northern Kingdom. Bethel is mentioned as the site of his confrontation with a priest of Israel (7:10-17). Since Bethel was on the southern border of Israel, it was not far from Jerusalem on the north. God called Amos to preach in Israel. We do not know how that happened, except the Lord told Amos to do this (v. 15).

Amos did his work **in the days of Uzziah king of Judah, and in the days of Jeroboam the son of Joash king of Israel.** Since both Uzziah [uh-ZIGH-uh] and Jeroboam II had long reigns, this statement does not narrow down the time very much. Uzziah's reign over the Southern Kingdom of Judah was from 792-740 B.C., and Jeroboam's reign over the Northern Kingdom of Israel was from 793-753 B.C. Verse 1 helps with the date by mentioning that Amos preached **two years before the earthquake.** Our problem is that we don't know for sure when this particular earthquake occurred. Most Bible students date Amos's ministry sometime in the decade 760-750 B.C.

During this period of Israel's history, Syria and Assyria were not threatening Israel. Thus it was a time of peace and prosperity. The rich lived in luxury and exploited the poor. Religion flourished, but it was not the religion of the Lord. Amos saw the signs of coming judgment and cried out in warning. He did not confine his warnings to Israel, but pronounced judgment on the nations that surrounded Israel. His stern denunciations of sin in Israel went unheeded. The people rejected Amos and his message. Within a few years (722 B.C.) the Assyrians swept down on Israel and Israel ceased to exist as a nation.

1:2: And he said, The Lord will roar from Zion, and utter his voice from Jerusalem; and the habitations of the shepherds shall mourn, and the top of Carmel shall wither.

Verse 2 summarizes Amos's message. Lions hunt their prey quietly, but they terrify their victims with fierce roaring as they spring to make the kill. This fact is in the background of the words **the Lord will roar from Zion. Utter his voice** is sometimes translated "thunders" (NIV). The voice of the Lord is sometimes compared with thunder (see Ps. 29:3-9). **Zion** is the mount on which the temple in **Jerusalem** stood. The mention of the central and authorized place of worship was a means of rebuke for the Northern Kingdom's altars at Dan and Bethel. When Jeroboam the son of Nebat broke with Judah, he feared that the Israelites would be drawn back to Judah to worship. Therefore, he built these two places of worship. The Bible condemns him and his successors for this disobedience (1 Kings 12–13).

Habitations means "abodes." Since the abodes of shepherds were often in the pastures with their sheep, some translations use "pastures" (NIV). **Mourn,** when used for the land, often refers to some natural disaster (Hos. 4:3; Jer. 12:11). Since **wither** is used parallel to **mourn,** some translations maintain the picture of drought by speaking of the pastures drying up. In either case, the last part of verse 2 presents a picture of a severe drought. **The top of Carmel** refers to a very fertile part of the land. Amos predicted a drought so severe that even that area would wither.

The two pictures in verse 2 both present the proximity of judgment. The roar of a lion is heard as it attacks. The roll of thunder signals the approach of a storm. Ironically, this thunder preceded a time of drought. One of the deadly powers of sin is its ability to cause people to consider judgment as something far away either in time or distance. Amos and Hosea delivered to Israel God's final warnings of the proximity of judgment.

Pronouncement of Judgment (Amos 1:3-5)

What is significant about Amos pronouncing judgment on the nations? Can nations and other groups be held accountable for sins, or is the only accountability that of individuals? What formula did Amos use in declaring the guilt of each of the six pagan nations? What kind of sin was condemned in all six nations? What punishment was foretold for Aram?

1:3: Thus saith the LORD; For three transgressions of Damascus, and for four, I will not turn away the punishment thereof; because they have threshed Gilead with threshing instruments of iron.

Amos 1:3–2:3 was the first part of Amos's first sermon. In these verses he got the attention of the Israelites by condemning the sins of six surrounding nations: Syria, Philistia, Tyre, Edom, Ammon, and Moab. Other prophets also had sections on the sins of other nations, but Amos began with these. Taken as a group, these oracles show that God holds all nations accountable for certain basic moral standards. These nations were not as accountable as were Judah and Israel, with whom God had made a special covenant; however, they were condemned for basic sins against humanity.

This testifies to the biblical view that God is sovereign over His entire universe. This sovereignty extends beyond Israel and Judah to all nations. They are His by right of creation, and He has revealed Himself at least partially to all people. After the flood, God made a covenant with all nations through Noah. Part of this covenant was the value of each human life (Gen. 9:6). Sins against humanity thus are sins against the God who created all human beings in His own image.

The Bible emphasizes individual accountability for sin, but nations, families, churches, and other groups are accountable in their own way. People do things as part of a group that they might not do on their own, but they are still responsible and have their part of the guilt. Many of the war criminals after World War II pleaded not guilty because they were only following orders. God sent Israel and Judah into exile for the sins of their nations. This does not mean there were not people of true faith in these nations. The prophets spoke of the faithful remnant, but the sins of a nation can bring divine judgment on the entire nation.

Each of these six judgments is preceded by the words **thus saith the LORD** (1:3,6,9,11,13; 2:1). Amos was clearly speaking here for God. Each judgment began with the formula **for three transgressions . . . and for four, I will not turn away the punishment thereof.** The numbers **three** and **four** do not refer to literal numbers of sins. Rather, the formula seems to mean that their sins were overflowing in number. The last part of the formula is literally, "I will not turn it back." The *King James Version* adds the word **punishment,** assuming that "it" refers to punishment. The idea is the divine law of sin and retribution (Num. 32:23; Gal. 6:7). Sin carries within it the seeds of its own destruction.

Each of the six pagan nations was condemned for sins of inhumanity. The people of Syria, of which **Damascus** was the capital, were guilty of atrocities against the people of **Gilead.** This was an area of the east side of the Jordan where some Israelites settled. The people of Damascus **threshed Gilead with threshing instruments of iron** ("sledges having iron teeth," NIV). **Threshing** was done by animals pulling huge stones or sledges of iron over the grain. Some of the sledges had iron spikes. Apparently the Syrians used these sledges as terrible instruments on helpless people, perhaps prisoners of war. Our world, with all its so-called enlightenment, continues to have all kinds of atrocities against innocent people: torture of political prisoners, persecution of Christians, acts of genocide, and so forth.

1:4-5: **But I will send a fire into the house of Hazael, which shall devour the palaces of Ben–hadad. [5]I will break also the bar of Damascus, and cut off the inhabitant from the plain of Aven, and him that holdeth the scepter from the house of Eden: and the people of Syria shall go into captivity unto Kir, saith the LORD.**

These verses describe the judgment coming on **Syria,** which had been Israel's chief enemy for many years. **Hazael** and **Ben–hadad** were two Syrian kings. **House** may refer to a residence or to a line of descendants. **Palaces** probably refers to "fortresses" (NIV), "strongholds" (NRSV), or "citadels" (NASB). All the things in which the Syrians trusted for national defense would be destroyed.

I will break the bar of Damascus refers to the "gate bar" (NKJV) that kept the huge city gate barred against enemies. Cities in that day were protected by high, strong walls and heavy gates locked with iron bars. The strongest walls were no protection if the bar of the main gate was broken. Enemies could enter and defeat the people of any such city. **The inhabitant**[s], the king—**him that holdeth the scepter from the house of Eden**—and **the people of Syria shall go into captivity.** This prediction literally became true when the revived Assyrian Empire overran Syria and captured Damascus in 732 B.C., a decade before the fall of Israel to the same enemy forces.

Grounds for Judgment (Amos 2:4-8)

For what sins were the people of Judah condemned? How did the Israelites feel when they were listening to the lists of sins of the nations and of Judah? How did they feel when Amos turned to naming their sins? Which of Israel's specific sins had to do with exploitation? What other sins were condemned?

2:4-5: **Thus saith the Lord; For three transgressions of Judah, and for four, I will not turn away the punishment thereof; because they have despised the law of the Lord, and have not kept his commandments, and their lies caused them to err, after the which their fathers have walked:** ⁵**But I will send a fire upon Judah, and it shall devour the palaces of Jerusalem.**

Amos was from **Judah**; therefore, he was familiar with the sins of Judah. He did not hold back from condemning his own people. Amos used the same formula from the six other nations in introducing the specific sins of Judah. Again he said, **Thus saith the Lord.** He also used the same words about **transgressions.** However, he mentioned more than one sin, and he mentioned sins that grew out of Judah's covenant relationship with God.

First of all, the Lord said, **They have despised the law of the Lord.** When God entered into a covenant with the children of Israel, they agreed to obey His **commandments**; however, they had not done this. Their second sin was that **their lies caused them to err. Lies** refers to "false gods" (NIV). In other words, they had sinned in the two areas in which they were supposed to show their covenant relation with God. They were to have a distinctive faith in one God and to have a distinctive way of living based on His commandments. The people of Judah had turned from the one true God to many false gods, and they had compromised their distinctive way of life by becoming like other nations who knew not God. In doing this they were following the sinful ways of **their fathers.**

Notice that Judah was more accountable for her sins than the nations that had no covenant with the Lord. The greater the opportunity, the greater the accountability.

2:6-7: Thus saith the Lord; For three transgressions of Israel, and for four, I will not turn away the punishment thereof; because they sold the righteous for silver, and the poor for a pair of shoes; ⁷that pant after the dust of the earth on the head of the poor, and turn aside the way of the meek: and a man and his father will go in unto the same maid, to profane my holy name.

How do you think the people of Israel who heard Amos's sermon were feeling before he spoke verses 6-8? Very likely they approved of, perhaps even took delight in, the condemnation of the pagan nations, who had been their enemies or rivals. They probably also felt smug when Amos condemned his own nation of Judah.

Amos was led by God to use this strategy to draw a crowd and to get their attention. Then when they were saying "amen" to what he was saying, Amos suddenly turned his guns on them. Amos used the same introductory words he had used in the previous seven condemnations, except this time it was directed against **Israel.** Verses 6-8 mention more kinds of sins than were mentioned in the previous seven condemnations. Verse 10 uses "you," showing that these words were for them. What were their sins?

First, **they sold the righteous for silver. Righteous** here refers to innocent people who were in the right. The word **sold** makes many Bible students think that the sin was selling into slavery people who owed debts they could not pay. The wealthy creditors callously sold these fellow Israelites into slavery for the money they received in payment from those who bought the slaves. This practice transgressed the law about humane treatment of slaves (Ex. 21:2-11). Parallel to this first line are the words **and the poor for a pair of shoes.** If this is only another way of saying the same thing (as Hebrew parallelism often is), the point is that the righteous poor were sold for such a trifling amount as a pair of shoes. Another way to interpret these words is to apply them to injustices in courts. The **silver** then represents bribes by the rich and powerful to get judgments against the poor and helpless members of society.

Several ways have been proposed to translate the words **that pant after the dust of the earth on the head of the poor**: "They trample on the heads of the poor as upon the dust of the ground" (NIV); "They . . . trample the head of the poor into the dust of the earth" (NRSV). One way to paraphrase the idea is to say that they treated the poor like dirt.

What happened when the exploited sought justice or help? The powerful **turn aside the way of the meek** ("deny justice to the oppressed," NIV; "push the afflicted out of the way," NRSV). The Old Testament clearly teaches certain things about the responsibility of God's people toward the helpless, the poor, and the afflicted. First of all, no one is to mistreat others so that they become poor and afflicted. Second, they are not to exploit any other person or group. Third, they are to help and defend the poor and helpless. The Israelites of Amos's day had failed on all three counts. Some callous people enslaved and impoverished others, taking advantage of their plight. Even the better members of society failed to care enough to stand up for the rights of others.

In addition to these sins of injustice, exploitation, and indifference, the Israelites were guilty of sexual immorality: **A man and his father will go in unto the same maid.** To what did this refer? Three possibilities have been suggested. (1) This may have been a father and his son who went to one of the Baal worship services and had sexual relations with the same temple prostitute. (2) It may have been that a father and a son both took advantage of the same female slave in their household. (3) It may have been that a father had sexual relations with his son's wife or a son had sexual relations with his stepmother. Any one of these actions would break the clear biblical teaching about sex as the means for a husband and wife to express responsible, lasting love for each other in the one-flesh union of marriage. Such sins **profane** God's **holy name.**

2:8: **And they lay themselves down upon clothes laid to pledge by every altar, and they drink the wine of the condemned in the house of their god.**

This verse brings together four sins in one: exploitation, idolatry, sexual immorality, and callous indulgence.

It was a sin of exploitation because the guilty parties kept **clothes** that were given by a debtor as a **pledge** of payment. The Old Testament is careful to give the benefit of the doubt to the debtor. A creditor could ask for a pledge of payment, but he could not keep a poor person's garment overnight (Ex. 22:26-27; Deut. 24:12-13). Keeping such a pledge overnight deprived the poor of what served as cover at night. Thus this was another example of exploitation.

It was an expression of idolatry since the sinners laid down **by every altar . . . in the house of their god**. Even if the last part of verse 7 does not refer to temple prostitution, verse 8 deals with worship at pagan altars.

It was a sin of sexual immorality, for the best explanation of the word **lay** is sexual sin. "The lying down . . . seems to have involved sexual immorality fueled by drunkenness."[2]

Wine of the condemned probably refers to "wine taken as fines" (NIV). The wine was a fine for debt or payment of taxes. In either case, it was not intended to be used in the way described here.

Forewarning and Scope of Judgment (Amos 3:7,13-15)

What role did prophets play? What was Bethel and what was its judgment? How was the luxurious self-indulgence of the rich to be judged?

3:7: Surely the Lord GOD will do nothing, but he revealeth his secret unto his servants the prophets.

After seven cause-and-effect questions in 3:2-6, Amos wrote of the special relation of the Lord's revelation and the task of the prophets. Verse 7 shows three things about this. First, God does not keep all His ways secret. Second, He makes them known by revelation. That is, people do not discover God; God reveals Himself. Third, God often uses **prophets** as His **servants** in making known His word.

3:13-15: Hear ye, and testify in the house of Jacob, saith the Lord GOD, the God of hosts, [14]that in the day that I shall visit the transgressions of Israel upon him I will also visit the altars of Beth–el: and the horns of the altar shall be cut off, and fall to the ground. [15]And I will smite the winter house with the summer house; and the houses of ivory shall perish, and the great houses shall have an end, saith the LORD.

Israel is called **the house of Jacob** in verse 13. The full name of God is used in this solemn warning of judgment: **the LORD God, the God of hosts.** The forewarning of judgment applied to **Beth–el.** This place was a noble place in the time of the patriarchs. Jacob particularly was connected with this place, which means "the house of God" (Gen. 28:19; 35:1). But after the kingdom divided, King Jeroboam built an altar there. This altar was corrupted by pagan elements and practices. All of the prophets had condemned this worship. Amos was no exception. He foretold its destruction **in the day** when the Lord would **visit the transgressions of Israel upon him** ("punish Israel for their transgressions," NKJV). Specifically, God would punish **the altars of Beth–el. The horns of the altar** would **be cut off. Horns** on the four corners of an altar held sacrifices in place. The horns also came to signify the sanctuary or safety one could claim by clinging to the horns of the altar (1 Kings 2:28). By destroying the horns, the Lord would end the use of Bethel's altars for sacrifices and would remove Beth–el as a place of refuge.

Verse 15 focuses on the sins of the self-indulgent rich. Only the wealthy people could afford a **winter house** and a **summer house. Houses of ivory** refers to the use of expensive ivory in these homes of the rich and famous of that day. **Ivory** is mentioned in 6:4, in a passage that describes the self-indulgence of the rich of that time. **Great houses** can refer to large mansions or to many different houses.

❖ *Spiritual Transformations*

In "Search the Scriptures" we have seen the proximity of judgment for Israel in the picture of a roaring lion. As an example of God's judgment on the nations, we saw Syria condemned for the sin of inhumanity. We heard the grounds for judgment against Judah and Israel. We looked at the warning of judgment coming on Israel's houses and place of worship.

No one likes to be confronted by the truth that each of us is accountable to God and will face divine judgment. The lost will be condemned and punished. Even believers must give account of how we have lived when we stand before the judgment seat of Christ (2 Cor. 5:10). How ready are we for that searching judgment?

Are you sure you know Christ and have been saved from the second death of eternal separation from God? _____

If you had to face the searching judgment of God today, of what would you be ashamed? _____

Prayer of Commitment: Lord, help us to be sensitive to our own sins, to confess them, and to forsake them. Amen.

[1]Billy K. Smith, "Amos," in vol. 19B of *The New American Commentary* [Nashville: Broadman & Holman Publishers, 1995], 36-37.
[2]Smith, "Amos," NAC, 64.

EVIDENCES OF GENUINE RELIGION

Background Passage: Amos 4:1–6:14
Focal Passage: Amos 5:4-7,10-15,21-24
Key Verse: Amos 5:24

❖ *Significance of the Lesson*

• The *Theme* of this lesson is that true religion impacts daily living.
• The *Life Question* this lesson seeks to address is, How should I demonstrate my religion?
• The *Biblical Truth* is that genuine religion is evident in right treatment of others, especially the poor and less powerful members of society.
• The *Life Impact* is to help you demonstrate faith in God by compassionate, consistent, godly behavior.

Judgment and Mercy in Amos

In a secular worldview, religion—which is often viewed as a crutch for the weak-minded—is rejected. If viewed as valid at all, religion is perceived as isolated from and having no impact on daily living.

In the biblical worldview, true religion—or genuine faith in God—should impact every aspect of our daily lives, especially our relationships with the poor and less powerful.

Word Studies: *Justice* and *Righteousness*

Justice and *righteousness* are key words and themes in the Book of Amos, especially in chapter 5. The *King James Version* generally translates the Hebrew word *mispat* as **judgment,** but most modern translations use "justice" (see 5:7,15,24). Sometimes the word does refer to "judgment" (as in Deut. 1:17), but more often "justice" is closer to the intended meaning. The companion word is *sedaqa,* or **righteousness,** which is often found used together with "justice." This pair is found, for example, in Amos 5:7 and 24. The two words obviously are closely related in meaning; however, each has some distinctives. *Mispat* has a judicial setting and often deals with justice in the courts of the land. *Sedaqa* means living in the right way because of allegiance to the righteous God. God is the One who is perfectly just and righteous (Ps. 103:6, NIV). Human justice and righteousness grow out of a right relation with God. Sinners practice injustice and commit sins. God, however, offers to forgive sinners and calls repentant sinners to practice His kind of justice and righteousness.

❖ *Search the Scriptures*

When Amos called the people to seek God and live, He was calling them to repent of their sins of injustice and unrighteousness. He warned against substituting anything for God, even religion. Amos condemned many specific sins in these two areas and called the people to seek good and not evil. God condemned the kind of religion that fails to change lives and called the people to let righteousness and justice flow like mighty rivers.

From this lesson we will learn three specifics about how we properly should demonstrate our religious faith.

Seek God, Not Substitutes (Amos 5:4-7)

*What does it mean to **seek** God? How is life conditioned on seeking God? What substitutes for seeking God do people use? What is the alternative to seeking God? How did the people sin against God's standards of justice and righteousness?*

Verses 4-5: For thus saith the Lᴏʀᴅ unto the house of Israel, Seek ye me, and ye shall live: ⁵But seek not Beth–el, nor enter into Gilgal, and pass not to Beer–sheba: for Gilgal shall surely go into captivity, and Beth–el shall come to nought.

Here is another passage that begins with the words **thus saith the Lᴏʀᴅ.** Verse 4 quotes God Himself: **Seek ye me, and ye shall live** ("Seek Me and live," NKJV). **Seek** translates a Hebrew word that has the idea of searching for something in order to verify it personally. In this case, they were to seek God Himself. He promised that if they did seek Him, they would **live.** This is significant because the chapter began as a funeral lament over fallen Israel (see vv. 1-2). Israel was so far gone that she was as good as dead—unless she seized one last opportunity to seek the Lord. Then and only then would she live.

Notice they were to seek God Himself, not some substitute for Him. Verse 5 lists some of Israel's substitutes in Amos's time. They were warned to **seek not Beth–el.** This place had been hallowed by Jacob's experiences there centuries before (see Gen. 28; 35). However, Jeroboam the son of Nebat had built a pagan altar there. A similar situation existed in **Gilgal.** It also had a rich history, but it had become corrupted over the years. The third place mentioned was **Beer–sheba** at the southern end of Judah. Many wealthy Israelites liked to go there for religious retreats and pilgrimages.

In 4:4 Amos had used bitter irony in calling the people to "come to Beth–el, and transgress" and "at Gilgal multiply transgression." These religious shrines had become corrupted into sites for false religion. However, even if they had been places of pure worship, they could have become substitutes for seeking God. Some people substitute practices such as churchgoing for seeking God Himself. Imagine what Amos would say today. He might say, "Seek God, not your church sanctuary; at Ridgecrest or Glorieta double your sins." Going to these places is right and good, but only as they provide settings for seeking the Lord Himself. The basic issue for each of us is seeking God personally. When you go to church, do you seek God and meet Him in true worship?

Verses 6-7: **Seek the Lord, and ye shall live; lest he break out like fire in the house of Joseph, and devour it, and there be none to quench it in Beth–el. [7]Ye who turn judgment to wormwood, and leave off righteousness in the earth.**

In verse 4 God had called, **Seek ye me, and ye shall live.** In verse 6 the prophet repeated this call on behalf of the Lord, **Seek the Lord, and ye shall live.** Verse 6 also states the alternative to seeking God and living—it was to refuse to seek God and to die. **Fire** was a familiar Bible picture of divine judgment. **The house of Joseph** means the same as the house of Jacob or Israel. Joseph's two sons, Ephraim and Manasseh, became the forefathers of two of the most important tribes in the Northern Kingdom. Unless they sought the Lord, He would **break out like fire in the house of Joseph, and devour it, and there shall be none to quench it.**

Verse 7 focuses on their chief sin, which Amos has been condemning—they **turn judgment** ("justice," NKJV, NIV) **to wormwood** ("bitterness," NIV). This could also be translated, "You who turn justice upside down."[1] This is a graphic picture of what they had done. Instead of practicing God's kind of justice, they had done the exact opposite. Parallel to this was their sin of casting or throwing "righteousness to the ground" (NIV; **leave off righteousness in the earth**).

Seek Good, Not Evil (Amos 5:10-15)

Who were the hated and who were the haters in verse 10? What was the situation described in verse 11a? Why would they not be able to enjoy their mansions and vineyards? How do bribes make justice impossible? Who were **the prudent** *who should remain silent? What is the relation between seeking good and seeking God? Why do some people confuse good and evil? Whose responsibility is it to establish justice in the courts? How does the hope of a* **remnant** *reveal God's mercy?*

Verses 10-12: **They hate him that rebuketh in the gate, and they abhor him that speaketh uprightly. [11]Forasmuch therefore as your treading is upon the poor, and ye take from him burdens of wheat: ye have built houses of hewn stone, but ye shall not dwell in them; ye have planted pleasant vineyards, but ye shall not drink wine of them. [12]For I know your manifold transgressions and your mighty sins: they afflict the just, they take a bribe, and they turn aside the poor in the gate from their right.**

Hate and **abhor** express strong negative emotions. Who was hating whom? The haters were those who hated **him that rebuketh in the gate. The gate** was the city gate, which served in that day as a court in which cases were heard and decided by community leaders. Hence the *New International Version*'s rendering, "the one who reproves in court." The one who reproved others at the gate in this context refers to people who in a legal setting defended the poor against the injustices of others.

Those who planned to exploit the poor and helpless hated those who championed and defended them. They hated Amos and others who spoke out on behalf of the poor and exposed and condemned the sins of the rich and powerful.

Verses 11-12 illustrate some of the situations against which Amos and others spoke out. One of the ways of **treading . . . upon the poor** was practiced by wealthy and selfish landowners against the poor tenant farmers who worked their land. The **burdens of wheat** refers to the burden of having to give to the landowner most of the grain that had been planted and harvested by the poor. Thus the poor got poorer and the rich got richer. The rich were able to build **houses of hewn**

stone and to plant **pleasant vineyards** with the money and grain they unjustly took from the poor. Amos pronounced judgment on these callous exploiters. They would build mansions, but they would **not dwell in them.** They would plant huge vineyards, but they would **not drink wine of them.** Amos knew that judgment was just down the road for such sinners. The fine houses and rich vineyards would be destroyed or the owners would not be there to enjoy these tokens of the good life. These wealthy sinners were warned that they would face harsh judgment and not enjoy their ill-gotten riches.

In verse 12 these sinners were warned that God knew their **manifold transgressions and** their **mighty sins.** Then the prophet listed some specific examples. **The just** whom they oppressed were innocent and good people. One of the sins of the oppressors about which the Lord knew was that **they take a bribe.** This was one of the chief ways that they turned **aside the poor in the gate** ("deprive the poor of justice in the courts," NIV).

Daniel Webster said, "There is no happiness, there is no liberty, there is no enjoyment of life, unless a man can say, when he rises in the morning, I shall be subject to the decision of no unwise judge today."[2] There is no justice when a judge, a witness, or a juror acts on behalf of someone who has bribed him or her. Yet over the centuries people giving and other people accepting bribes—whether of money or of influence—have upset the delicate scales of justice. Unscrupulous people of wealth and power have been guilty. Greedy people who have taken bribes also have their share of guilt.

Verse 13: **Therefore the prudent shall keep silence in that time; for it is an evil time.**

Verse 13 has puzzled Bible students of all generations. There are questions about the meaning of the three parts of the verse: Who are **the prudent**? Why are they to **keep silence**? When was the **evil time**? **Prudent** translates the Hebrew word *sakal,* which generally refers to a person of insight and understanding. The **evil time** could refer to the evil time in which Amos lived and served, or it could refer to the coming time of judgment. The puzzle is why Amos would advise anyone to **keep silence** ("keep silent," NKJV) at a time when he himself was far from silent. This seems the only sure thing about the verse. Amos strongly condemned sin. Even when threatened, he faithfully and boldly told the truth in God's name. Therefore, he was far from being prudent. Perhaps then Amos was being ironic in this verse. He may even have been quoting a proverb with which he did not agree. Some Bible students think he may have been speaking of the coming time of divine judgment. If so, Amos may have been telling people to accept God's judgment quietly. "In that future time, the prudent person will quietly acquiesce to the judgment, since the prophetic word has so fully demonstrated both its certainty and its necessity. They who have silenced the claims of the innocent in court shall themselves be silenced by the inevitability of their own punishment."[3]

Verses 14-15: **Seek good, and not evil, that ye may live: and so the LORD, the God of hosts, shall be with you, as ye have spoken. [15]Hate the evil, and love the good, and establish judgment in the gate: it may be that the LORD God of hosts will be gracious unto the remnant of Joseph.**

What is the relation between seeking **good** (v. 14) and seeking **God** (vv. 4,6)? God is good, and He calls people to be good. Those who truly seek God also seek the good that comes through knowing and serving God. **Good** is the opposite of **evil.** Many people have confused the two. Isaiah warned, "Woe unto them that call good evil, and evil good; that put darkness for light, and light for darkness; that put bitter for sweet, and sweet for bitter!" (5:20). This is a frightening picture of the moral confusion of our own day, with its relative standards of right and wrong.

Those who seek God and good shall **live.** The promise to them is that **the LORD, the God of hosts, shall be with you.** They know the blessing of the only true life—that which comes through fellowship with God. The words **as ye have spoken** seem to refer to their claim that God was already with them. Amos promised that He would truly be with them only if they sought Him and lived the good life according to His standards.

Not only were they to **seek good, and not evil,** but they also were to **hate the evil, and love the good.** Amos gave them a practical example of what this would involve. In the area of justice, it would mean that they would **establish judgment in the gate** ("maintain justice in the courts," NIV). They were to become the champions of the kind of justice that many of them had hated (see v. 10). Amos's classic statement of this is in verse 24. Ernst Jacob noted, "The justice of Yahweh is not of the type of the blindfolded maiden holding a balance in her hand, the justice of Yahweh extends one arm to the wretch stretched out on the ground whilst the other pushes away the one who causes the misfortunes."[4]

If they were to seek God and good, then they in essence would be repenting. Establishing justice in the courts would be a fruit of their repentance. The call to repent is always based on the desire of the Lord to forgive sinners who turn from their sins to Him. When this happens, God is able to **be gracious** ("have mercy," NIV). Amos used a key Old Testament idea when he called such people **the remnant of Joseph.** The prophets realized that all of the people of national Israel were not truly God's people. Many of them were sinners who lived as did the sinners of other nations. The prophets pronounced judgment on both Israel and Judah. Both nations were defeated, and many of their people either were killed or made captives. However, the prophets realized that some of the people in these sinful nations were true to God. They loved and served Him in spite of all. Thus there was a faithful remnant of true children of God among the people.

Seek Righteousness, Not Ritual (Amos 5:21-24)

What Old Testament worship practices are mentioned in these verses? What negative words are used to describe how God felt about them? What kind of worship was God condemning: pagan, compromised, ceremonial, or hypocritical? If Amos were speaking to our generation, what might he say about our worship practices? What actions are needed to obey verse 24?

Verses 21-23: I hate, I despise your feast days, and I will not smell in your solemn assemblies. [22]Though ye offer me burnt offerings and your meat offerings, I will not accept them: neither will I regard the peace offerings of your fat beasts. [23]Take thou away from me the noise of thy songs; for I will not hear the melody of thy viols.

This is the third use of the word **hate** in this lesson. The exploiters hated the good people who rebuked them (v. 10). The godly were to hate evil (v. 15). Now God Himself is said to **hate** something. This is a strong word. Its parallel word **despise** is equally strong. We are accustomed to speaking of God's love, not His hatred. What could be so evil that God is said to hate it? The first-time reader of Amos might be surprised that God hated their religious worship practices. No doubt these words shocked the people of Amos's day! The prophet, claiming to speak for God, said, **I hate, I despise your feast days.** These could have been the feast days that God had ordained, such as Passover and Pentecost. These may have been other feast days added to the worship in the Northern Kingdom.

The *King James Version*'s **I will not smell in your solemn assemblies** seems odd to our ears today. The word **smell** in verse 21 refers to the Old Testament picture of sacrifices being a sweet smell to God. The newer versions are clearer: "I do not savor your sacred assemblies" (NKJV); "Nor do I delight in your solemn assemblies" (NASB). "I take no pleasure in your sacred ceremonies" (REB); "I cannot stand your assemblies" (NIV). Verse 22 lists three kinds of sacrifices taught in the Old Testament concerning the sacrificial system: **burnt offerings** (in which the entire animal was consumed on the altar), **meat** ("grain," NKJV, NIV, NASB) **offerings,** and **peace** ("fellowship," NIV) **offerings** (in which part of the animal was eaten by worshipers as a sign of communion with God). God said that although they offered these things, He would **not accept them.**

Music was a vital part of worship in the Old Testament. The Book of Psalms testifies to the use of hymns in worship. Yet the Lord said to **take . . . away from** Him **the noise of** their **songs.** Notice that the Lord called their songs **noise.** This was extended to include also their instruments of music. **Viols** or "harps" (NIV, NASB, NRSV; "stringed instruments," NKJV) were often used in their worship music. God said that He would not **hear the melody of** these.

Why did God use such strong negative words to describe His feelings about their worship? Were these worship practices condemned because they were acts of pagan worship? We know that at times the Israelites totally rejected the Lord and turned to idols. Verse 26 shows that some of this pagan idolatry was present in Israel. The gods of the Assyrians were worshiped. For us today, *pagan worship* is putting the gods of this world in the place of priority in our lives.

A second possibility is that the people claimed to worship God but actually worshiped other gods. When the Israelites made the golden calf, they claimed that the calf represented the god who delivered them from Egypt (Ex. 32:4). When Jeroboam the son of Nebat erected the altars at Dan and Bethel, he claimed that the calves were the means of worshiping the god who redeemed them (1 Kings 12:26-33). This may be called *compromised worship* practices. This is the kind of worship today that reflects the ways of the world rather than the ways of God.

A third possibility is that these were common ways of worshiping God under the old covenant but that the prophet opposed the sacrificial system as such. This can be called *ceremonial worship.* David believed in the temple system, but he realized that sacrifices could not take the place of repentance (Ps. 51:16-17). Micah said that the Lord did not require rivers of oil and many animal sacrifices, but that He wanted people to do justly, love mercy, and walk humbly with God (Mic. 6:6-8). This is the kind of worship today that makes ceremonies and worship actions take the place of worshiping God Himself.

The fourth possibility is that the prophet was not condemning the use of these worship practices but the attempt to use them to hide an evil way of living. The prophets and Jesus condemned such *hypocritical worship.* Many of the same words found in Amos 5:21-23 are also in Isaiah 1:11-17. Isaiah was not condemning sacrifices when conducted properly; what he was condemning was the ungodly living of those who went through the motions of worship. In Jeremiah's famous temple sermon he condemned those who thought that temple worship freed them to live an ungodly life (Jer. 7). Jesus condemned the Pharisees for hypocrisy, although many of their practices were biblical (Matt. 23). Jesus cleansed the temple—not because the temple was not divinely ordained for the old covenant—because the people were not living up to the expectations of the Lord. Worshipers of this kind use churchgoing to hide their sinful living.

"On a certain Sunday morning the Devil passed a church and paused to listen to the songs coming from within. . . . A passerby asked the Devil why he didn't go in and disrupt the service. 'Doesn't worship like this frighten you?' he asked. The Devil assured him that he wasn't at all disturbed, and as he left he was heard to say,

'They're praising God on Sunday;
They'll be all right on Monday,
It's just a little habit they've acquired.'"[5]

Amos also condemned greedy merchants who could hardly wait for the holy days to end so they could return to their stores, where they exploited the poor by selling inferior products at inflated prices (8:4-10).

What would Amos say about our worship practices? Is some of our worship *pagan*? Is some of our worship a *compromise* with the pagan world? Is some of it purely *ceremonial*? Is some of it *hypocritical*? In some cases he might condemn us for irreverent methods, but mostly he would condemn us for not practicing what we profess. Regular churchgoing and fervent worship cannot substitute for consistent, compassionate, godly living.

Verse 24: **But let judgment run down as waters, and righteous-ness as a mighty stream.**

Verse 24 is the strongest positive statement in the Book of Amos. It is a call for a life of **judgment** ("justice," NIV) and **righteousness.** Water is not plentiful in the land of Israel. Even the best springs and rivers often run slowly in dry seasons. The Lord called for a life of justice and righteousness that is like **waters** and **a mighty stream. Mighty** often is translated as "never-failing" (NIV, REB) or "ever-flowing" (NASB, NRSV). Justice and righteousness are to overflow in our lives and to keep flow-ing through good times and bad.

To move from where they were to where they should be called for the people of Israel to repent and to trust God for the grace and power of a new life. Such is the same for us today.

❖ *Spiritual Transformations*

In "Search the Scriptures" we have seen an emphasis on seeking God rather than seeking substitutes for the Lord and an emphasis on seeking good and hating evil. We also have seen a condemnation of hypocritical worship and a call for a life of overflowing and continuous justice and righteousness.

The positive emphasis of this lesson calls on believers to live a consistent, compassionate, and godly life. Seeking God and good are the keys. Justice and righteousness are the fruit.

*What would Amos say about your worship practices?*_____

_____

What would he say about how justice and righteousness are reflected in your life? _____

Prayer of Commitment: Almighty God, deliver us from false and hypocritical worship practices. Help us to seek You in genuine worship and to live for You in justice and righteousness. Amen.

[1]Douglas Stuart, *Hosea-Jonah,* in the Word Biblical Commentary, vol. 31 [Waco: Word Books, Publisher, 1987], 342.

[2]Carruth and Ehrlich, *American Quotations,* 309.

[3]David Allan Hubbard, *Joel and Amos,* in the Tyndale Old Testament Commentaries [Downers Grove: InterVarsity Press, 1989], 173.

[4]Ernst Jacob, *Old Testament Theology,* 99; cited by Hubbard, *Joel and Amos,* 168.

[5]Cited in Page H. Kelley, *The Book of Amos: A Study Manual,* in the Shield Bible Study Outlines [Grand Rapids: Baker Book House, 1966], 63.

COURAGE OF CONVICTION

Bible Passage: Amos 7:7-17
Key Verse: Amos 7:8

❖ *Significance of the Lesson*

• The *Theme* of this lesson is that faithfulness, or obedience, means doing what God says even when no one else does.
• The *Life Question* this lesson seeks to address is, Why should I take a stand for God in a society that is hostile to Him?
• The *Biblical Truth* is that God expects His people to remain faithful to Him even when they are vastly outnumbered by unbelievers.
• The *Life Impact* is to help you stand alone for God in the face of opposition.

Compromise or Conviction?

In the secular worldview, the safe and acceptable course of action is to go along with the majority, regardless of whether that majority is right or wrong. Some secular people have no convictions, some have evil convictions, and some have compromised convictions.

In the biblical worldview, God expects His people to adopt His standards as their own convictions. He further expects His people to have the courage to take a stand for Him based on those convictions, though taking such a stand may result in unpopularity, persecution, and death.

Word Study: *Plumbline*

The Hebrew word *'anak*, or plumbline, is found only four times in the Old Testament, all in Amos 7:7-8. A plumbline is "a string with a weight tied to the end of it" (CEV). It is used to ensure that a wall is perpendicular to the ground.

❖ *Search the Scriptures*

When God showed Amos the vision of the plumbline, God told the prophet that time had run out for Israel. Amaziah, the priest of Bethel, accused Amos of conspiracy against the king and told Amos to return to Judah to earn his living. Amos denied being that kind of prophet and pronounced judgment on Amaziah.

Certainty of Judgment (Amos 7:7-9)

How is the vision in verses 7-9 like and how is it different from the visions in verses 1-6? What was the message of the vision of the plumbline? How does the plumbline represent God's fixed standard? How does it represent the certainty of judgment?

Verses 7-9: Thus he showed me: and, behold, the Lord stood upon a wall made by a plumbline, with a plumbline in his hand. [8]And the LORD said unto me, Amos, what seest thou? And I said, A plumbline. Then said the Lord, Behold, I will set a plumbline in the midst of my people Israel: I will not again pass by them any more: [9]And the high places of Isaac shall be desolate, and the sanctuaries of Israel shall be laid waste; and I will rise against the house of Jeroboam with the sword.

The Book of Amos has two main parts: the oracles or messages in chapters 1–6 and the visions in chapters 7–9. The latter part has five visions, three of which are in chapter 7. All three begin by saying that these are what the Lord **showed** Amos (vv. 1,4,7). The first two parables present visions of coming judgments: locusts and fire. After each vision Amos prayed for the Lord to relent, and in each case He did (vv. 3,6). This shows that Amos was not a negative, vindictive Judean who wanted to see Israel punished; it also shows the Lord's persevering love for His sinful people.

However, the third vision shows the Lord's patience had worn out. Amos saw that **the LORD stood upon a wall made by a plumbline.** Most translations have the Lord "standing by" (rather than **upon**; NIV, NASB, REB) the wall. "The word 'standing' (*nissab*, a Niphal reflexive, i.e., 'station oneself') connotes a posture of firmness and determination, thus providing a contrast to the change of heart attributed to Yahweh in the first two parts of the vision."[1] Most translators assume that this wall "had been built true to plumb" (NIV; "vertical," NASB).

Others think that the wall was a leaning wall representing Israel. In either case, the point of the plumbline is clear. God was going to use that fixed standard to judge the uprightness of Israel.

The lasting biblical truth in **I will set** ("I am setting," NIV, NKJV) **a plumbline in the midst of my people Israel** is that God has a fixed standard. This is totally different from the modern view that wrong and right are relative to the person and situation. Many people do not believe in a fixed standard for human conduct, but the Bible clearly teaches it here and elsewhere.

God is merciful, not wanting any to perish, but all to come to repentance (2 Pet. 3:9); however, there is a point of no return for those who persist in violating His standard. This is the meaning of the words **I will not again pass by them any more** ("I will spare them no longer," NIV; "I won't forgive them any more," CEV). The nation had had many calls to return to the Lord, including the messages of Amos, but they had resisted them all. God already had charged, "I raised up of your sons for prophets, and of your young men for Nazarites. Is it not even thus, O ye children of Israel? saith the LORD. But ye gave the Nazarites wine to drink; and commanded the prophets, saying, Prophesy not" (2:11-12). Now they had rejected God's message through Amos. Thus, their doom was sealed.

Amos thus pronounced the Lord's judgment. The local shrines and places of worship were called **high places.** They were usually places of pagan worship and were consistently condemned by the prophets. **Isaac** is another way of referring to the Northern Kingdom of Israel, who took pride in their ancestry from Isaac. **The sanctuaries of Israel** were the shrines at Bethel and Dan, which Jeroboam the son of Nebat had set up to keep the people from going to the temple in Jerusalem. They were supposed to be places of worshiping the Lord, but their worship had been compromised in many ways. These two kinds of worship sites would **be desolate** and **laid waste.**

Amos also pronounced judgment on **the house of Jeroboam.** This was directed not only against Jeroboam II himself but also against his family and dynasty. Jeroboam II's son Zachariah was assassinated after six months, and Israel fell to the Assyrians (2 Kings 15:8-10). This word of judgment seems to have been the basis for Amaziah's later charge of conspiracy against Amos (see v. 10).

The positive lesson of this vision to believers is our need to live according to God's fixed standard, which is set forth in His Word. This is the reason we never graduate from Sunday School. We need to continually evaluate our lives in light of God's fixed standard. Then we need to readjust our lives so we live by His standard. We also must be willing to proclaim God's Word as the standard by which we are to live and by which God will judge all humanity.

We need to have convictions based on God's fixed standard in His Word. Convictions within themselves can be good or evil. Sidney Harris made a good point when he said, "I am tired of hearing about men with the 'courage of their convictions.' Nero and Caligula and Attila and Hitler had the courage of their convictions—but not one had the courage to examine his convictions, or to change them, which is the true test of character."[2] Having convictions is evil if the convictions are evil.

Some people have no real moral and spiritual convictions. When faced with moral challenges, they are swept along by whatever wind is blowing. Peter Marshall prayed:

> A man is a fool when he dies for his opinions.
> A man is a saint when he stands for his convictions.
> Give us clear vision that we may know where to stand and what to stand for, because unless we stand for something, we shall fall for anything.[3]

The lessons of verses 7-9 are these: (1) There is a fixed standard of right and wrong. (2) God's Word is that standard. (3) God's people should live by that standard and base their convictions on it. (4) Those who reject the standard or consistently break it will be judged.

Conflict of Loyalties (Amos 7:10-17)

*What was Amaziah's position and source of authority? What charge did he make against Amos? Was the charge true? Why did he call Amos a **seer**? What did Amaziah tell Amos to do? How did he describe Bethel? How do verses 10-13 illustrate the attacks people make on those who live by God's standards?*

Verses 10-13: Then Amaziah the priest of Beth–el sent to Jeroboam king of Israel, saying, Amos hath conspired against thee in the midst of the house of Israel: the land is not able to bear all his words. [11]For thus Amos saith, Jeroboam shall die by the sword, and Israel shall surely be led away captive out of their own land. [12]Also Amaziah said unto Amos, O thou seer, go, flee thee away into the land of Judah, and there eat bread, and prophesy there:

¹³but prophesy not again anymore at Beth–el: for it is the king's chapel, and it is the king's court.

Beth–el was the site of the shrine that Jeroboam the son of Nebat had built in the southern part of Israel. It was probably the place where Amos did much of his preaching. He certainly mentioned it often in his messages (see also 4:4; 5:5-6). For the first time in Amos, we are introduced to **Amaziah the priest of Beth–el.** Verse 10 introduces the only narrative portion of the Book of Amos. Here is the confrontation between the priest of Bethel and the prophet from Judah, who had been preaching in Israel. The passage shows that Amaziah was a kind of hired priest or court priest, whose allegiance was to the king. He was no doubt paid by the king. He had sold out to the powers that be and lived to do their bidding.

Amaziah **sent to Jeroboam king of Israel,** who was probably in Samaria the capital of Israel. The phrase suggests a runner with a verbal or written message. This **Jeroboam** was Jeroboam II, who is described in 2 Kings 14:23-29. He was successful in enlarging the borders of Israel, but he perpetuated the sin of Jeroboam the son of Nebat. Amaziah accused Amos of a serious crime in any nation. He charged that Amos had **conspired against** the king. In other words, Amos was accused of plotting against the king. He was said to be guilty of coming into Israel and conspiring against the government. The word is *qasar,* which means "tie up," "be allied together," or "form a conspiracy." Jeremiah was accused of the same crime against his native land of Judah (Jer. 26:11; 37:11–38:4). Jesus was accused of treason against Rome and officially crucified on this false charge (Luke 23:2).

The charges against Amos, Jeremiah, and Jesus were groundless. None of these was guilty of political sedition. Amos had indeed pronounced judgment on the house of Jeroboam, but he was not a part of any political plot to assassinate the king. Jeremiah had predicted the fall of Judah to Babylon, but he was not part of a plot to achieve this. Jesus did claim to be a King, but He was not leading a rebellion against Rome.

Amaziah accused Amos of predicting that **Israel shall surely be led away captive out of their own land.** This was true (see 6:14), but this would be the result of God's judgment, not the result of Amos's conspiracy.

Amaziah informed the king that **the land is not able to bear all his words. Bear** translates *kul,* which means to "hold," "contain," or "endure": "The country cannot tolerate what he is saying" (NEB); "Our nation cannot put up with his message for very long" (CEV).

We do not know whether Jeroboam replied to Amaziah's message. If he did, verse 13 may represent his reply. If he did not reply, it was not out of unconcern but because the king knew that Amaziah would say what Jeroboam wanted him to say.

Amaziah began by calling Amos a **seer** (*hozeh*), using one of two Old Testament words for **seer.** Many Bible students believe that *hozeh* means the same thing as the word **prophet** (*nabi'*)in verse 14. In support of this view is the fact that the verb *naba* for **prophesy** is found with both words. Another point in its favor is that verses such as Isaiah 29:10 use the words synonymously. Many others believe that *hozeh* was used in a derogatory sense by Amaziah. They think that Amaziah used it to charge Amos with seeing things in visions that were not true. Today, we would say, "He's seeing things!"

Although we cannot know for sure how Amaziah was using the word **seer,** likely his words to Amos were derogatory. He had slandered him in his message to the king. He definitely threatened him in what he said in verses 12-13: **Go, flee thee away** ("Get out, you seer! Go back. . . ." NIV). **Flee** translates *berah,* which has the idea of "run for your life." Amaziah may have ridiculed him with the word **seer.** He certainly ridiculed him by telling Amos to return to his native **Judah, and there eat bread, and prophesy there. Eat bread** means "earn your living" (NEB, REB). Amaziah was accusing Amos of preaching for pay. Ironically, this was the sin of which Amaziah himself was guilty. He had sold himself to Jeroboam the king. Amaziah accused Amos of perhaps being an agent of the king of Judah, who paid him to come north to upset Israel.

Acting on his authority, and thus on the king's also, Amaziah ordered Amos to **prophesy not again anymore at Beth-el.** The priest may not have had the authority to arrest Amos, but he did claim to have the authority to order him to leave the country. The allegiance of Amaziah to Jeroboam is seen in his description of Bethel as **the king's chapel** and **the king's court.** In other words, this was supposed to be a place to worship the Lord, but it actually was a place to honor the king. The place belonged to Jeroboam, not to the Lord.

Verses 10-13 contain several relevant lessons for us. First of all, these verses illustrate how those who do not live by God's standards attack those who stand up for God's way. Some people attack prophets because they have compromised their own convictions. Amaziah was a case in point. The attacks are designed to slander, to ridicule, or to intimidate people of true convictions. Sometimes all three motives are involved. Therefore, when people of faith take a stand on the basis of convictions growing out of God's Word they can expect to face one or more of these kinds of attacks. People of the Bible faced such difficulties. Amos was not alone. Nebuchadnezzar threatened Daniel's three friends with death if they refused to bow down to his idol (Dan. 3). Jesus was repeatedly attacked by His enemies. So were the apostles and the believers of the early centuries. So are many people in our world today—especially those in non-Christian lands that oppose Christianity.

A missionary from the International Mission Board in one of the last frontier areas tells of a man whose name is withheld because of the risk to him. "A few years ago 'E' was one of the 99.9 percent of his people who are Muslim and have never met someone who was not. Now 'E' is one of the handful of believers who publicly identify themselves as followers of Christ. Despite being monitored by the security force, 'E' is living for Christ. He has led some to faith, including two religious leaders. Pray for a hedge of protection around him, for he knows that his days of freedom may be numbered."

The courage of people such as "E" shames many Americans who keep quiet about their faith in our land of religious freedom and many professing Christians. People in our land do not face persecution of the same kind and intensity, but believers sometime find themselves in situations in which they are slandered, ridiculed, and/or threatened. Do we have the convictions needed to stand up and speak out for the Lord?

Verses 14-17: **Then answered Amos, and said to Amaziah, I was no prophet, neither was I a prophet's son; but I was an herdman, and a gatherer of sycamore fruit: [15]and the LORD took me as I followed the flock, and the LORD said unto me, Go, prophesy unto my people Israel. [16]Now therefore hear thou the word of the LORD: Thou sayest, Prophesy not against Israel, and drop not thy word against the house of Isaac. [17]Therefore thus saith the LORD; Thy wife shall be an harlot in the city, and thy sons and thy daughters shall fall by the sword, and thy land shall be divided by line; and thou shalt die in a polluted land: and Israel shall surely go into captivity forth of his land.**

Why did Amos deny that he was a prophet? How did he earn his living? Why was he preaching in Israel? How did Amaziah's words conflict with the words of God? What judgments did Amos pronounce on Amaziah? How did Amos illustrate the courage of one person with convictions?

A literal translation of verse 14 does not have any verbs: "No prophet I, and no son of a prophet I; but a herdsman I, and a dresser of sycamores." Therefore, each translator must decide whether the verb is past ("was") or present ("am"). Some follow the *King James Version* and use **was** (NIV, NKJV, REB). Others such as the *New American Standard Bible*, use "am": "I am not a prophet, nor am I the son of a prophet" (see also NRSV, NEB).

If "am" is correct, then Amos was denying that he was at the time or ever had been a prophet. The problem with this is that Amos spoke so highly of prophets in 2:11 and 3:7. Also, both Amos and Amaziah used the verb *naba*, which means **prophesy.** The noun for **prophet** in verse 14 is *nabi*, the most common Old Testament word for the office.

If **was** is correct, Amos was saying, "Before my call came, I was not a prophet; neither had I been trained in one of the schools of the prophets." That seems to be the meaning of denying being **a prophet's son.** There were groups of prophets called "sons of the prophets" (2 Kings 4:38). Amos thus was admitting that he was a prophet, but he was denying that he was a professional prophet. He strongly denied that he preached for pay as Amaziah had charged.

We cannot be sure whether Amos was referring to the past or present, but one thing is clear: He denied being the kind of professional prophet who served a king because the king provided him with food— "I am not the kind of prophet who prophesies for pay" (GNB/TEV).

How had Amos earned his living? He said that he was a *boqer.* Some translate this as "shepherd" (NIV), basing their translation on the words **I followed the flock.** Others use **herdman** ("herdsman," NASB, NRSV, REB, NEB) or "sheepbreeder" (NKJV). He also said that he was **a gatherer of sycamore fruit.** The word *boles* seems to have designated more than just a fruit picker. He "took care of sycamore-fig trees" (NIV). He was "a dresser of sycamore trees" (NRSV). Stuart commented: "There is some uncertainty about the precise meaning of these terms . . . and it has also been suggested that Amos uses them not literally but as self-effacing terms (e.g., 'Shucks, I'm just a country farmer') to indicate that Amaziah had nothing to fear from him. The evidence suggests, however, that Amos intends to identify himself as one who had no financial reason to prophesy at Bethel or anywhere else."[4]

Amos said that the reason for his prophesying in Bethel was that the Lord called him to do that: **The Lᴏʀᴅ said unto me, Go, prophesy unto my people Israel.** Amaziah was telling him, **Prophesy not against Israel.** Who was Amos to obey—the Lord or Amaziah? The words of Amaziah were exactly the opposite of what the Lord had called Amos to do. Amaziah ordered Amos to leave Israel and return to Judah. Amos, however, followed the authority of the Lord, not that of Amaziah or of Jeroboam.

Amos was moved by that kind of inner compulsion that comes from a clear call of the Lord. He was like Jeremiah who, when he tried to be silent, was not able to do so because there was a fire in his bones (Jer. 20:9). He was like the apostles who, when ordered not to preach anymore in the name of Jesus, said they could not fail to tell the things they had seen and heard (Acts 4:20). In speaking of this compulsion, Amos had written in 3:8: "The lion hath roared, who will not fear? the Lord Gᴏᴅ hath spoken, who can but prophesy?"

Faced with threats from Amaziah, Amos stood up and spoke out. He even dared to pronounce judgment on his attacker. He predicted that the priest's wife would become a prostitute, his children would be killed, and he would **die in a polluted land.** All of these tragedies would happen when **Israel** was taken **into captivity.** Although this did not happen right away, the judgment was sure to come in God's own time.

The lesson here is the "Life Impact" of standing alone for God in the face of opposition. Although all those about us attack us, we should have the courage of our convictions and call from God. Just as the Bible and history are filled with examples of people of faith who were slandered, ridiculed, or threatened, so are they filled with examples of people of courage who stood up and spoke out for God—Jeremiah, the three Hebrew young men, Daniel, John the Baptist, Jesus, Stephen, Paul, Martin Luther, John Bunyan, William Carey, John G. Paton, Roger Williams, and many more.

Roger Williams came to Massachusetts Bay Colony seeking religious freedom. Ironically, the Puritans, who had come to be free from the restrictions of the Church of England, founded a repressive government in the new world. Williams, by contrast, believed that no civil authority could dictate faith or religious practices. He taught that faith is a matter between God and the individual. The state should not demand or control religion. He was brought before the civil authorities and asked if these were his beliefs. He affirmed that they were. Thus he was exiled from Massachusetts, and he went and began a new colony where people were free to worship. He founded Rhode Island and the city of Providence.

John G. Paton was an 18th-century missionary to the islands of the South Pacific. Cannibals lived there, and they had killed several missionaries. They repeatedly threatened to kill Paton, but he did not leave. He stayed and continued to preach, eventually leading some to Christ. Then these converts and the missionary were all under constant danger of being killed. Paton claimed the Lord's promise of His abiding presence at the end of the Great Commission.

> I'll go where You want me to go, dear Lord,
> O'er mountain or plain or sea;
> I'll say what You want me to say, dear Lord,
> I'll be what You want me to be.[5]

❖ *Spiritual Transformations*

In "Search the Scriptures" we saw the vision of the plumbline and its interpretation. We also saw the confrontation between Amaziah, the priest of Bethel, and Amos, the prophet of the Lord.

The three main points of the lesson are these: (1) God has a fixed standard by which He judges people. (2) Those who reject God's standards attack those who seek to live by them. (3) Those who believe in God's standards must stand up and speak out for God, even if they must sometimes stand alone.

In what kind of situations are you attacked because of your Christian faith? _____

How do you respond to such attacks? _____

Prayer of Commitment: Lord, give us the courage of convictions based on Your Word and Your call. Amen.

---

[1]Thomas Edward McComiskey, "Amos, Micah," in vol. 7 of *The Expositor's Bible Commentary* [Grand Rapids: Zondervan Publishing House, 1985], 321.

[2]Quoted in Roy B. Zuck, ed., *The Speaker's Quote Book* [Grand Rapids: Kregel Publications, 1997], 87-88.

[3]Quoted in Zuck, *The Speaker's Quote Book*, 87.

[4]Stuart, *Hosea–Jonah*, 377.

[5]Mary Brown, "I'll Go Where You Want Me to Go," *Baptist Hymnal* [Nashville: Convention Press, 1956], No. 425.

PROMISE OF RESTORATION

Background Passage: Amos 8:1–9:15
Focal Passage: Amos 8:11-12; 9:5-15
Key Verses: Amos 9:13-14

❖ *Significance of the Lesson*

• The *Theme* of this lesson is that even in judgment, the Lord offers hope through a promise of restoration.
• The *Life Question* addressed by this lesson is, Is there a future beyond the Lord's judgment?
• The *Biblical Truth* is that the sovereign Lord offers hope beyond judgment.
• The *Life Impact* is to help you depend on God who restores His people.

Judgment and Hope

In the secular worldview, the biblical warnings of God's judgments are usually met with unbelief or unconcern.

In the biblical worldview, believers take seriously God's warnings of judgment and His words of hope.

Prophets Proclaimed and Predicted

Many people think of the Old Testament prophets primarily as people who predicted future events. They did some of this, but they were primarily preachers of God's word to their own generation. Their preaching emphasized judgment on human sin, but it also contained calls for mercy based on divine love. The predictions concerning the future were often warnings of judgments coming on the generation to which they preached; however, the prophets also made predictions of events beyond their own generation. Many of these predictions have been fulfilled already, but some remain unfulfilled. Much of the prophets' preaching and their predictions focused on Israel, but they also focused on people of other nations.

Word Study: *The tabernacle of David that is fallen*

The background to the phrase **the tabernacle of David that is fallen,** found in Amos 9:11, is the promise of God to David that one of his descendants would reign over an everlasting kingdom. The kings of Judah were descendants of David, but none of them fulfilled what God promised to David in 2 Samuel 7. When Judah fell to the Babylonians, the people ceased to have a king. During those dark centuries the "tent" (NIV; "booth," NRSV, NASB; "house," NEB, REB; "kingdom," CEV) of David was like a fallen building. Amos, however, promised that it would be rebuilt. This was a way of reassuring the people that the Messiah-King would still come.

❖ *Search the Scriptures*

One of the judgments on Israel would be a famine of hearing God's word. Almighty God is sovereign over not only Israel but also over the Gentiles. God would shake Israel like a sieve, so that only the faithful remnant would be spared while all the sinners would be judged. God would rebuild the fallen house of David and restore the people to a land of rich and fertile fields.

Severity of Judgment (Amos 8:11-12)

*How does this word of judgment fit into the message of the chapter? What kind of famine did Amos predict? When was this to happen? What does Deuteronomy 8:3 show about the need for the word of God? What is the meaning of the words **from sea to sea**? Why will people seek the word of the Lord so frantically? How does this apply to our own time?*

8:11-12: Behold, the days come, saith the Lord God, that I will send a famine in the land, not a famine of bread, nor a thirst for water, but of hearing the words of the Lord: [12]and they shall wander from sea to sea, and from the north even to the east, they shall run to and fro to seek the word of the Lord, and shall not find it.

Like many of Amos's predictions, chapter 8 focuses on warnings of sure and severe judgment. This fourth vision (the first three were in chapter 7) depicts the corruption and rottenness of Israel as a basket of overripe fruit. God's judgments in this vision were compared to an earthquake and flood (v. 8), a solar eclipse (vv. 9-10), and a famine concerning the word of God (vv. 11-12). Earlier, in 4:6, Amos had predicted a literal famine of food: "I also have given you cleanness of teeth in all your cities, and want of bread in all your places" ("I gave you empty stomachs in every city and lack of bread in every town," NIV). Now he predicted a different kind of famine. The **famine** predicted in 8:11 would be **not a famine of bread, nor a thirst for water, but of hearing the words of the LORD.**

The people of Israel had many opportunities to hear and respond to the word of the Lord through His prophets. They had told the prophets to be silent (2:12). Amos himself had been told by the priest of Bethel to leave the country (7:12-13). Their punishment for rejecting the word of the Lord was that they would no longer be able to hear the word of God through His prophets.

In the background of this terrible prediction is the truth of the human need for the word of the Lord. Shortly after the beginning of Israel's history, as Israel prepared to enter the promised land, Moses reminded them how the Lord had fed them during the years in the wilderness. He also spoke His word to them. The Lord's long-range purpose was to teach them and all later generations of believers that "man doth not live by bread only, but by every word that proceedeth out of the mouth of the LORD" (Deut. 8:3). Jesus, of course, quoted these words to the devil when He was tempted to turn stones into bread (Matt. 4:4). The point of this key verse is that just as food and water are essential for physical life, so is the word of the Lord essential for moral and spiritual life. Being deprived of His word results in moral and spiritual starvation.

These later Israelites also had thought that they didn't need the word of the Lord. But when the voice of the prophets was silenced, some of them would begin to realize their desperate plight. Amos predicted that **they shall wander from sea to sea, and from the north even to the east.** This was one way of referring to all four directions. The Dead Sea was to the south and the Mediterranean Sea was to the west of Israel. Thus **from sea to sea** means from south to west. When this is put with **from the north even to the east,** we have all four points on the compass.

Amos was writing about a series of judgments coming "in that day" (8:9,13). He began verse 11 with the words **Behold, the days come.** Amos used "in that day" in verse 13 in describing the results of the famine on young men and women. To what day was he referring? In Amos 5:18, the prophet wrote about "the day of the Lord." The callous people were daring the Lord to send that day, but Amos warned them that it would be a day of judgment and darkness, not of light. "The day of the Lord" in the Bible refers at times—as here—to earthly days of judgment. In other places in the Old Testament and in the New Testament the phrase refers to the final day of the Lord (see 2 Pet. 3:10). In the case of the Northern Kingdom of Israel, the use of the phrase likely refers to the time of destruction by the Assyrians when Israel ceased to exist. However, the judgment of absence of the word of God happens whenever a nation or people reject the message of God's word.

In some lands, the government has forbidden its people to have Bibles or to preach the good news. As a result, they have a hunger and a thirst that nothing else can satisfy. Many of the people do not recognize the reason for this famine of the spirit, but others realize that it is a famine of the absence of the word of the Lord. We have seen this since the breakup of the Soviet Union and the fall of Communism in eastern Europe. Many people have hungrily sought Bibles and listened to the preaching of the Word of God.

Those who refuse to hear God's word eventually are punished by no longer being able to hear it. In our own land, many refuse to read the written Word of God or to hear those who declare God's Word. They are headed for a famine of the soul as a result of this rejection. Theirs is a self-imposed famine of the spiritual food that only God's Word can provide.

Inevitability of Judgment (Amos 9:5-10)

*Why is verse 10b the key to Amos 9:1-10? How does the doxology of verses 5-6 apply to Israel's problem? What is amazing about verse 7 in light of the rest of the Old Testament? What is **the sinful kingdom**? Who are those whom the Lord promised to save and not destroy when judgment came? How do these truths address the people described in the last part of verse 10?*

9:5-6: And the Lord God of hosts is he that toucheth the land, and it shall melt, and all that dwell therein shall mourn: and it shall rise up wholly like a flood; and shall be drowned, as by the flood of Egypt. ⁶It is he that buildeth his stories in the heaven, and hath founded his troop in the earth; he that calleth for the waters of

the sea, and poureth them out upon the face of the earth: The Lord is his name.

The key to Amos 9:1-10 is in the last part of verse 10. Many of the Israelites were saying that **the evil shall not overtake nor prevent us.** They claimed to be immune to any judgment of God because they were God's chosen people and He would never destroy His own people. This presumptuous attitude was similar to the view of the people of Judah in Jeremiah 7. As Jeremiah later did, Amos spoke the word of the Lord that condemned His people for their sins and pronounced inevitable judgment on them.

This fourth vision in 9:1-4 shows the Lord standing beside the altar. Then follows a series of warnings that there would be nowhere for the people to hide from the wrath of their God.

Verses 5-6 constitute the third doxology in the Book of Amos (see 4:13; 5:8-9). It begins and ends with the name of the Lord: He is **the Lord God of hosts** ("the Lord, the Lord Almighty," NIV), and **the Lord is his name.** These titles emphasize Him as the covenant God of Israel and also as the sovereign Lord of all people and things. He is **he that toucheth the land, and it shall melt.** Billy K. Smith thought these words probably described an earthquake: "The verb translated 'melts' (*mug*) probably is better rendered 'trembles' or 'quakes,' since the rest of the hymn contains earthquake imagery (cf. Ps 75:3 [Heb., 75:4]; Nah. 1:5). Earthquakes cause so much death and destruction that entire populations may be thrown into mourning."[1] The last part of verse 5 is similar to 8:8. The comparison is to the rising and falling of the Nile River. This can picture the movement of the earth during an earthquake. We cannot say for sure that verse 5 describes an earthquake, but we can say for sure that it depicts the control of the sovereign Lord over His creation.

Verse 6 pictures God as sovereign in the heavens and on the earth. He controls **the waters.** He can send forth the life-giving rain, and He can send forth the death-dealing storms and floods.

Douglas Stuart pointed out how verses 5-6, probably part of an ancient hymn extolling God's power over nature and people, spoke to the presumption of Israel: "In effect he [Amos] says: 'That hymn you love shows how Yahweh controls the universe and metes out his judgment among the nations. But you have wrongly assumed that this judgment would always benefit you and harm others. Now you must realize that *you* also deserve the wrath of which the hymn speaks.'"[2]

9:7: **Are ye not as children of the Ethiopians unto me, O children of Israel? saith the LORD. Have not I brought up Israel out of the land of Egypt? and the Philistines from Caphtor, and the Syrians from Kir?**

This is one of the most amazing verses in the Old Testament. It affirms the fact that the Lord has been active in the affairs of all nations, not just of the people of Israel. Amos already had shown that the sovereign God judges the nations as well as Israel (chaps. 1–2). Now he showed that the Israelites were not the only people to be loved or the only ones to be led to and given a special land as an inheritance. The inspired words written by Amos affirm God's love for **the Ethiopians** ("Cushites," NIV). The Jews did not have much regard for the people of this distant land, but the Lord said, "The Ethiopians are no less important to me than you are" (CEV).

Then the prophet mentioned two nations that had been enemies of Israel. Just as the Lord had **brought up Israel out of the land of Egypt,** so He had brought up **the Philistines from Caphtor** [KAP-thawr—that is, the island of Cyprus], **and the Syrians from Kir.** While God was at work dealing with the people of Israel, He also had moved in the affairs of other nations to bring to pass His purpose. His purpose always had included not just the Israelites but also people of all nations. Nevertheless, this did not render these nations immune to God's judgment (see 1:3-5 and 1:6-8 respectively for the judgments on these nations).

The point of verse 7 in answering the presumption of the Israelites in verse 10 was that Israel stands on the same ground as do all nations. God loves all people, but He will spare none who persistently sin against Him. God's involvement with the nation of Israel did not make them any more immune to judgment than His involvement with other nations made them immune to judgment.

9:8-10: **Behold, the eyes of the Lord GOD are upon the sinful kingdom, and I will destroy it from off the face of the earth; saving that I will not utterly destroy the house of Jacob, saith the LORD. ⁹For, lo, I will command, and I will sift the house of Israel among all nations, like as corn is sifted in a sieve, yet shall not the least grain fall upon the earth. ¹⁰All the sinners of my people shall die by the sword, which say, The evil shall not overtake nor prevent us.**

What was **the sinful kingdom**? It was the nation of Israel as a political entity. **The eyes of the Lord GOD** were **upon** it, and He said that He would **destroy it from off the face of the earth.** This prediction came true in 722 B.C., when Assyria defeated Israel, killed many, and scattered most of the rest of the people of Israel among the nations.

The last part of verse 8, however, contains a word of hope. **I will not utterly destroy the house of Jacob, saith the LORD.** Some Bible students think that **the house of Jacob** refers to the people of Judah, the Southern Kingdom; however, earlier in the book Amos referred to Israel by the name **Jacob** (6:8; 8:7). Thus the ones who would not be destroyed seem to have been the faithful ones in the nation of Israel. This does not mean that they did not suffer some of the results of being in the sinful nation, but it does mean that these individuals had sought the Lord and thus would live (5:4).

This mixture of judgment and hope continues in verse 9. God would **sift the house of Israel among all nations.** He was using the analogy of a farmer who sifts his grain to separate the good grain from the impurities and chaff. The good grain sifted through and was preserved. The larger chaff and pebbles were separated from the good grain.

All the sinners of my people shall die by the sword were the ones who said, "Disaster will not overtake or meet us" (NIV). Verses 1-10 show the deceptiveness and deadliness of such presumption. Sin deceives people who think that all is well because of some favored relation with God. The people of Israel were chosen, but many of them thought of this as being chosen only for blessings and privileges, not also for mission and responsibility. This self-deception proved deadly in the end.

Verses 8-9 provide a note of hope beyond judgment. This emphasis is expanded in verses 11-15. No matter how bad things get, believers can have hope based on the mercy of the Lord for His faithful people. Such assurance based on hope is different from presumption based on status.

Promise of Blessings (Amos 9:11-15)

How can we answer those who say that Amos was a prophet of doom who would not have written such words of hope? According to the New Testament, what was the fulfillment of verses 11-12? What is described in verses 13-15? What are the various views about how this will be fulfilled? What aspects of hope do all believe? What difference does such hope make in how believers live?

9:11-12: In that day will I raise up the tabernacle of David that is fallen, and close up the breaches thereof; and I will raise up his

ruins, and I will build it as in the days of old: [12]**that they may pos-sess the remnant of Edom, and of all the heathen, which are called by my name, saith the Lord that doeth this.**

In that day refers to a time future to the people of Amos's day. Earlier Amos had used it of a day of judgment; here he used it of hope beyond judgment. Some Bible students feel that Amos was a prophet of doom who could not have written such words of hope. This overlooks two facts: First, Amos earlier had given a few glimpses of hope based on God's mercy. He called on the people to seek the Lord and live (5:4). He spoke of a remnant to be saved (5:15; 9:8). He twice prayed for God to spare the people, and twice the Lord relented (7:1-6). Second, nearly all the Old Testament prophets preached hope beyond judgment.

Amos quoted God as saying that He would **raise up the tabernacle of David that is fallen** (see the "Word Study"). David's dynasty is pictured as a fallen "booth" (NASB, NRSV). The Lord promised to see it raised up, to repair its holes, and to rebuild it to be what it once was.

God had promised to David a descendant who would reign over an everlasting kingdom. Descendants of David ruled the Southern Kingdom of Judah, but none of them fulfilled this promise. Judah outlasted Israel by more than a century, but finally it also was defeated, its temple destroyed, and its king and his family made captives. For centuries, there was no king of David's line. The New Testament says that Jesus Christ fulfilled the promise God made to David. Jesus is the Messiah-King of David's line, and He has established a reign in human hearts that is eternal. He will also bring His kingdom and His people to a consummation at the time of His future coming.

Thus the fulfillment of verses 11-12 was in Jesus Christ and the carrying out of His purpose for His people and for all people. God's purpose for His people was **that they may possess the remnant of Edom, and of all the heathen** ("Gentiles," NKJV; "nations," NIV, NASB, NRSV), **which are called by** the Lord's **name.** The fact that this would be the work of the Lord is seen in the words **saith the Lord that doeth this.**

Amos 9:11-12 is quoted in the New Testament. At the Jerusalem Council, James quoted it as scriptural support for the inclusion of Gentiles in the church on the same basis with Jewish believers. He thus followed Simon Peter in supporting the missionary work of Paul and Barnabas and disagreeing with some of his fellow Jews that Gentiles had to become Jews before they could be saved. The quotation is in Acts 15:15-17. James quoted here from the Greek translation of the Old Testament, called the Septuagint. Thus the New Testament explains Amos 9:11-12 as being fulfilled in Jesus Christ's leadership in including Gentiles as well as Jews among His people.

9:13-15: Behold, the days come, saith the LORD, that the plowman shall overtake the reaper, and the treader of grapes him that soweth seed; and the mountains shall drop sweet wine, and all the hills shall melt. [14]And I will bring again the captivity of my people of Israel, and they shall build the waste cities, and inhabit them; and they shall plant vineyards, and drink the wine thereof; they shall also make gardens, and eat the fruit of them. [15]And I will plant them upon their land, and they shall no more be pulled up out of their land which I have given them, saith the LORD thy God.

These verses predict a time of future fertility and abundance in the land to which the people had returned from **captivity**. Verse 13 stresses the abundance. Under normal conditions, the task of the **plowman** and the **reaper** were several months apart. The same was true of the time between the work of the **treader of grapes** and **him that soweth seed.** Amos predicted a time when they would come together. He also predicted that **the mountains** would **drop sweet wine.**

In verse 14 Amos predicted the return of Israel from captivity and their restoration to the land. God would bless them in many ways. The greatest blessing as stated in verse 15 would be that the Lord would **plant them upon their land** and that they would **no more be pulled up out of their land which** the Lord had **given them.**

Most Bible students agree that this and similar Old Testament prophecies of Israel's return to the land were only partially fulfilled with the return from exile during Old Testament times. Most believe that the ultimate fulfillment is still future and will take place in connection with the return of the Lord. As regarding the Book of Revelation, there are several schools of thought about the number and timing of the events that will take place. Some feel that this promise will be fulfilled in an earthly kingdom in which Jews will have the prominent role. Some believe that the fulfillment will include an earthly millennium in which both believing Gentiles and Jews who are the people of God will take part. Still others believe that this prophecy is symbolic of the time when all believers will take part in the new heavens and new earth. The central reality on which all agree, however, is that God's people have confident hope based on the promises of God's Word.

Recently someone lent me an old book on World War II. As I read the early chapters, I realized that much attention was given to events leading up to the war. This led me to look at the end of the book. I discovered that the last event mentioned was the Battle of the Coral Sea. I quickly turned to the copyright page and found that the book was published in 1942. Most of the war news prior to that time had been a series of Axis victories. Yet to take place were Midway, Guadalcanal, Stalingrad, D-Day, and other Allied victories that led to final victory. Things looked grim in May 1942; yet the last page in the book forecast victory because of the potential of combined efforts of the United States, Great Britain, and the Soviet Union.

We know what the final outcome of World War II was because we see it from the side of victory. The plight of the world and the people of God in the world at times look grim. However, we know what the final outcome will be. The Lord will be victorious over evil, and His faithful people will share in His eternal kingdom. We know this because we believe the promises of God in His Word.

❖ *Spiritual Transformations*

Amos predicted a famine of the hearing of the word of the Lord. He attacked those who presumed they never would face divine judgment. He predicted hope beyond judgment.

This study has several lessons for life. One is that those who reject or ignore the Word of God condemn themselves to a time when they can no longer hear it. Another is that those who presume that they will not face judgment are wrong. A third lesson is that beyond judgment is the hope based on faith in the Lord.

What difference in your life does it make because you believe that judgment is inescapable? _____

What difference does your hope in the Lord make in your life? _____

_____

Prayer of Commitment: Lord, deliver me from the sin of presumption and help me to live in light of Your promises. Amen.

[1]Smith, "Amos," NAC, 158.
[2]Stuart, *Hosea-Jonah*, 392.

Study Theme

Being God's Agent in Crisis Times

"The Chinese character for crisis consists of two characters. The top character means danger, and the bottom character means opportunity."[1] This four-session study theme focuses on the following kinds of crises: sickness, death, and bereavement; storms and natural disasters; destructive dissension in a church; and persecution of Christians. The victims of these crises in the four Bible studies were a 12-year-old girl and her father, 276 people on a small sailing ship, the church at Corinth, and Peter and the church in Jerusalem.

The word *agent* refers to a person who represents someone else in a specific matter. The word is used in this study of those who represent God in some crisis situation. The agent of God in dealing with sickness and death was none other than Jesus, the Son of God. He was God's agent in the ultimate sense. The agent or representative of God in dealing with the storm at sea was Paul, who himself was one of the 276 threatened by the storm. Paul was also God's representative in trying to help the Corinthian church avoid worse dissension. The agents representing God in the persecution of the church and their leader Peter were the members of the church itself.

How did each agent represent God in these crisis times, and to what degree can we learn from their examples? Jesus was able to do for Jairus and his daughter something we cannot do for the sick, the dying, and the bereaved. We cannot restore the dead to life, but we can pray for and comfort those who are in these crises. Paul prayed for and gave assurance to those caught in the storm at sea. So can we in the midst of the storms that enter people's lives. Paul prayed, wrote, and visited the Corinthian church to help them become one in spirit. We too can seek to help our church and other churches maintain unity of spirit in the bond of peace. The church prayed for Peter, and that is one thing we can do for the thousands of believers who are being persecuted all over the world today.

[1]Zuck, *The Speaker's Quote Book*, 93.

MINISTRY IN PHYSICAL CRISIS

Background Passage: Mark 5:21-43
Focal Passage: Mark 5:21-24a,35-43
Key Verse: Mark 5:36

❖ *Significance of the Lesson*

• The *Theme* of this lesson is that Jesus, through His example, teaches us how to help others in times of physical crisis by being sensitive to need, encouraging faith, and showing compassion.

• The *Life Question* addressed in this lesson is, How can I help others in times of sickness and death?

• The *Biblical Truth* is that Jesus is our model for helping others in times of sickness and death by being sensitive to needs, encouraging their faith, and showing them compassion.

• The *Life Impact* is to help you minister to others in times of sickness and death.

Responses to Sickness and Death

Adults struggle to know how to respond to people who are experiencing physical crises. Many adults are uncomfortable with making visits to hospitals and funeral homes because they do not know what to say and do in those situations. Those who have a secular worldview also fear their own death.

In the biblical worldview, believers have a model of how to help people when they see how Jesus helped people in His day. They learn from Him how to be sensitive, to encourage faith, and to show compassion.

Word Study: *Sleepeth*

The word translated **sleepeth** in Mark 5:39 is *katheudei*. At times this word was used in the New Testament to describe literal sleep (see 4:38). At other times it was used to describe the dead as sleeping. Jesus told the disciples that his friend Lazarus had fallen asleep and that He was going to wake him up. The disciples thought that Jesus meant that Lazarus was only asleep. Then Jesus explained that Lazarus was dead (John 11:11-14). Even secular people of that day spoke of death as being asleep. They usually meant that dead people often look as if they are only asleep. When used of physical death, *katheudei* hints at the awakening from the dead.

❖ *Search the Scriptures*

Jairus came to Jesus and asked Him to come and lay His hands on his dying daughter so she might live. Jesus went with him. Some people came to Jairus and told him that his daughter was dead and that he need not trouble Jesus further. Jesus urged Jairus not to fear but to keep believing. When He got to the house, Jesus told the mourners not to grieve because the girl was not dead but asleep. When they laughed at Him, He put them out. Then Jesus took three of His disciples, along with the parents of the girl, into where the girl's body was. He spoke the word, raised her up, and told her parents to feed her.

Notice the people and groups that are mentioned in this story: Jesus, His disciples, the "inner circle" of three disciples, the crowd, Jairus, his wife, his daughter, the messengers who told Jairus that his daughter was dead, and the mourners. Jesus showed how to act when others are sick, dying, or bereaved. Jairus showed how to act when a loved one is sick, dying, or dead. The messengers and the mourners showed how not to act.

Jesus Was Sensitive to Need (Mark 5:21-24a)

When and where did this event take place? What people and groups are in the Focal Passage? What do we know about Jairus? Why did he come to Jesus? How did Jesus respond to his request?

Verses 21-24a: **And when Jesus was passed over again by ship unto the other side, much people gathered unto him: and he was nigh unto the sea.** [22]**And, behold, there cometh one of the rulers of the synagogue, Jairus by name; and when he saw him, he fell at his feet,** [23]**and besought him greatly, saying, My little daughter lieth at the point of death: I pray thee, come and lay thy hands on her, that she may be healed; and she shall live.** [24]**And Jesus went with him.**

Jesus had been on the eastern side of the Sea of Galilee when He healed the demoniac (4:35; 5:1-20). Now He **passed over again by ship unto the other side.** This means that He came to the west or northwest side of the body of water. Most likely He was near Capernaum, where He had earlier performed miracles (1:21-28; 3:1-7) and where He forgave the man lowered through the roof (2:1-12). As had been true earlier, **much people gathered unto him** ("a large crowd gathered around him," NIV). Also, as earlier, many of His actions took place **nigh unto the sea** (1:16; 2:13; 3:7; 4:1).

What do we know about **Jairus**? He was an important man in the community. He was **one of the rulers of the synagogue,** probably the one in Capernaum. A ruler of a synagogue was the chief administrator of the synagogue. He planned the worship services and invited the speakers. He administered the financial affairs and material undertakings of the synagogue. Because Capernaum was a leading city of the region, being one of its rulers was a prestigious job.

Some Bible students assume that as the leader of the synagogue at Capernaum Jairus shared the views of those religious leaders who were opposed to Jesus (2:7,16,24; 3:6,22). Certainly Jairus knew what Jesus had done in the synagogue and in Capernaum. He had to have some knowledge about Jesus' reputation as a healer in order to come to Him with his own deep need. If he had held negative attitudes toward Jesus, he laid them aside when he came to Him. He came to Jesus humbly, desperately, and with faith.

Jairus was an important (and thus probably a proud) man, but he totally and publicly humbled himself when he came to Jesus. He humbled himself when **he fell at his feet.** It is also said of Jairus that he **besought him greatly** ("pleaded earnestly with him," NIV). What brought this important man to Jesus? Jairus quickly stated his desperate need. He blurted out, **My little daughter lieth at the point of death.** Later we learn that his daughter was 12 years old. Even if Jairus's daughter might have objected to being called **little,** her father still saw her as his little girl. Like all good fathers, he had tried to be there for her; but, like all fathers, he had learned as she grew up that he could not always solve all her problems for her.

When our four children were small, I thought I could always be there for them. As they grew, I realized I never had always been there for them. The more they grew toward adulthood, the stronger was the realization that, as much as I wanted to be, I could not always be there when they needed help. I realized I must entrust them, as I did myself, into the care of our Heavenly Father, who is always there for each of us.

The account leaves no doubt that Jairus loved his little daughter. He was frantic because her life was ebbing away and there was nothing he could do. If you are a parent, you know how you feel when your child is sick, especially if the illness is serious.

Jairus heard that Jesus was back. Thus he came to Jesus and made his plea: **Come and lay thy hands on her, that she may be healed; and she shall live.** Jairus knew of Jesus' reputation as a healer, and he believed that Jesus could heal his dying daughter. His prayer was a mixture of faith and desperation.

Notice that no word of Jesus to the man is recorded. Instead, we simply are told that **Jesus went with him.** That action speaks volumes. Jesus, sensing the desperate plight of the girl and the faith of her father, went with Jairus toward his house. Jesus was sensitive to human needs. He often was interrupted in what He was doing by someone with a deep need. Even while He was on His way to Jairus's house, Jesus was delayed by the desperate woman who touched His garments hoping to be healed. Jesus was sensitive to this woman's need for healing, and He stopped to heal her.

What applications to life do we find in these verses? We see in Jesus' actions two lessons. First of all, He listened sensitively to Jairus's words. Second, He went with Jairus to do what He could to help. Jesus set us an example of how to respond when others are sick. For his part, Jairus did the right thing in taking the prayers for his sick child to Jesus. Further, Jairus came to Jesus with humility and faith.

If we are to minister to human needs, we need to have sensitivity to the needs of others. Some people are so intent on maintaining their own schedules and meeting their own needs that they are indifferent to the cries for help all about them. The Spirit of the living Lord leads others on daily missions of help for the needy people they encounter. True sensitivity leads us to act on behalf of those in need. Some people are uncomfortable in the face of the sickness and death of others. I've heard people say that they don't go to the hospital to visit the sick or to funeral homes to comfort the bereaved. They try to find excuses for failing to act. Often the excuse is that there is nothing we can do. We can't heal the sick or call the dead back to life. They say, "I don't know what to say." Sometimes our presence is more important than what we say. This is particularly true in dealing with the bereaved.

Jesus Encouraged Faith (Mark 5:35-36)

What news did the messengers bring to Jairus? What were their motives? How did Jesus respond to their words?

Verses 35-36: While he yet spake, there came from the ruler of the synagogue's house certain which said, Thy daughter is dead: why troublest thou the Master any further? [36]**As soon as Jesus heard the word that was spoken, he saith unto the ruler of the synagogue, Be not afraid, only believe.**

While he yet spake refers to the words Jesus spoke to the healed woman (vv. 25-34). Some people **came from the ruler of the synagogue's house.** We are not told who they were. They could have been friends, relatives, or others. All we know is what they said. They said two things, both addressed to Jairus. First, they said to Jairus, **Thy daughter is dead.** Delivering such news is never easy. There is no good way to tell a father that his beloved daughter is dead. However, there seems to be a lack of tact and concern in how these messengers bluntly informed Jairus.

The second part of their message was even more negative. Still addressing Jairus, they asked, **Why troublest thou the Master any further? Master** is *didaskalon*, the word for "teacher." There is no evidence that these messengers believed Jesus was anything more than a teacher. They certainly did not believe He could do anything for a dead person. And they tried to spread their unbelief to Jairus. Some Bible students think that these messengers represented either family or friends of Jairus who had been opposed to his going to Jesus in the first place. In their question, the word translated **troublest** is *skullo.* "The word *skullo,* from *skulon* (skin, pelt, spoils), means to skin, to flay. . . . Then it comes to mean to vex, annoy, distress."[1] The messengers suggested that Jairus would only be annoying Jesus if he still insisted on Jesus going to his house.

How did Jesus respond to this act of throwing cold water into Jairus's face? James A. Brooks commented on verse 36: "The first verb can mean either 'ignoring' (NIV, RSV), 'paid no attention to' (GNB), or 'overhearing' (NRSV, NEB, REB, NASB). The question arises whether Jesus rejected the report as false or whether he urged the ruler to believe despite his daughter's death. . . . The best explanation is that Jesus overheard what the messengers said and accepted the reality of the child's death but that he refused to accept the finality of death."[2]

We can only imagine how Jairus felt during this message and during Jesus' response. No doubt he was shocked and deeply grieved by the message that his daughter was dead. He may even have been tempted by their suggestion to send Jesus on His way. These messengers exemplify one of the wrong ways of dealing with the sick and the families of the sick and bereaved. They were callous in their timing and in what they said. Rather than encouraging faith, they discouraged it.

By contrast, Jesus set the positive example by encouraging faith. Before Jairus could respond to the messengers, Jesus spoke directly to him. He told him two things: First He said, **Be not afraid.** Jairus had been living in fear since his daughter became so sick. Second, Jesus said, **Only believe.** This is in a tense of the Greek verb that means ongoing action (the present imperative). Jairus had exercised faith when he came to Jesus. The Lord told him to continue to believe. Jesus did not explain why Jairus should believe nor did He tell Jairus what He intended to do. He simply told him to keep on believing.

To summarize, here's some of what these verses teach about sickness, dying, and death. The messengers show how not to respond to the death of someone's loved one. The messengers discouraged faith and acted callously with the bereaved. Jesus by contrast encouraged the shocked and grieving father not to fear but to keep on believing. Jairus listened to Jesus and did what He said.

How can you help to encourage the bereaved to keep believing? First, know that your presence with them can help. Second, avoid any trite sayings. Third, if you speak, tell them you love and care about them, read the Scriptures with them, and pray with and for them.

Jesus Showed Compassion (Mark 5:37-43)

Why did Jesus take only three of His disciples into where the girl was lying? Who was causing the tumult at Jairus's house? What did Jesus say to them? What did He do with them? What did He mean by **sleepeth***? How did He go about restoring the girl to life? Why did He ask them to tell no one about this miracle?*

Verses 37-40: And he suffered no man to follow him, save Peter, and James, and John the brother of James. [38]And he cometh to the house of the ruler of the synagogue, and seeth the tumult, and them that wept and wailed greatly. [39]And when he was come in, he saith unto them, Why make ye this ado, and weep? the damsel is not dead,

but sleepeth. [40]And they laughed him to scorn. But when he had put them all out, he taketh the father and the mother of the damsel, and them that were with him, and entereth in where the damsel was lying.

Peter, and James, and John the brother of James are called the "inner circle" of the disciples. On this occasion, at the transfiguration (9:2), and in Gethsemane (14:33), Jesus took only these three apostles with Him. He knew that these three, especially Peter and John, would play key roles in continuing His mission.

Each culture has its own ways of dealing with death. In first-century Jewish society, one of their customs was to have mourners weep and wail. Often these mourners were professional mourners. These professionals knew everyone in the community and their dead loved ones. Thus by calling out the names of the dead, they could get everyone weeping. Along with the mourners were the flute players (see Matt. 9:23). A later Jewish source stated that every funeral should have a least two flutes and one mourner.[3] Many more probably came to the house of a well-to-do person such as Jairus. These people must have been expecting the child to die because they had come so soon after her death. Perhaps they were already there when she died.

The Bible describes the scene that Jesus found in Jairus's house: He **seeth the tumult, and them that wept and wailed greatly** ("Jesus saw a commotion, with people crying and wailing loudly," NIV). Herschel H. Hobbs wrote: "The word for 'wailed' is an onomatopoetic word, a word whose very sound is related to its meaning. It is *alalazo,* to repeat over and over the cry *alala.* It was used by soldiers entering battle. The word is also found in 1 Corinthians 13:1 of a 'tinkling' [or clanging] cymbal."[4]

Jesus asked them, **Why make ye this ado, and weep?** Then He stated, **The damsel is not dead, but sleepeth.** Some people think that Jesus used the word **sleepeth** literally, meaning that she was only in a coma from which she would recover; however, the biblical account leaves no doubt that she was dead. Jesus used the word to point to the fact that she would be awakened from the sleep of death.

The supposed mourners showed how false their own motives were by their response to Jesus' words. And Jesus showed the same thing by what He did with them. **They laughed him to scorn. Laughed** translates a word meaning "to laugh at" with the prefix "down." Thus it has the idea of ridiculing. This showed not only their lack of faith in Jesus but also their insincerity as mourners. This is understandable if they were paid to weep and wail. They were good at doing this, no matter who had died. They apparently felt little real concern for Jairus and his grieving wife. Their indifference was in sharp contrast to Jesus' compassion.

Jesus dealt sternly with these make-believe mourners. The word translated **put them . . . out** is *ekbalon,* which was used of His casting out evil spirits (1:39), and it is the word used of what Jesus did with those who were buying and selling in the temple (Matt. 21:12). In other words, Jesus "showed them the door" or "kicked them out." He had no patience with pretense and hypocrisy. Jairus and his wife needed people with them who sincerely cared about them and could identify with them in their grief.

The professional mourners exemplify one of the wrong ways to deal with bereaved people—intruding on their sorrow to make money for themselves. There is nothing wrong with mourning and with weeping in times of sorrow. In fact, Paul wrote that believers ought to rejoice with those who rejoice and weep with those who weep (Rom. 12:15).

Jesus then took Jairus, Jairus's wife, Peter, James, and John with Him into the room where the girl's body **was lying.**

Verses 41-43: **And he took the damsel by the hand, and said unto her, Talitha cumi; which is, being interpreted, Damsel, I say unto thee, arise. ⁴²And straightway the damsel arose, and walked; for she was of the age of twelve years. And they were astonished with a great astonishment. ⁴³And he charged them straitly that no man should know it; and commanded that something should be given her to eat.**

Jesus held the dead girl's hand and said, **Damsel, I say unto thee, arise.** Mark gave the Aramaic words that Jesus actually used: **Talitha cumi** [tal-ih-thuh-KOO-mih]. Immediately the girl **arose, and walked.** This is where we are told that **she was of the age of twelve years.** Those in the room with Jesus **were astonished with a great astonishment.** This included the three disciples. Jesus told them not to tell this to others, although the people who knew she had died must have realized something wonderful had happened. Jesus did not want to be known primarily as a miracle worker. This could lead to many followers who went with Him only for what He could do for them.

The story closes with Jesus commanding that **something should be given her to eat.** This practical touch shows that Jesus was sensitive to the health and well-being of the girl who had been so sick. It suggests another way that many ladies help others who have sick loved ones or who have lost loved ones. Taking food to a family at such a time is a practical form of Christian ministry.

Jesus' actions show us that the death of a believer is not the end. He shows us that He has dominion over death. He comforted the bereaved parents by restoring their daughter to them. Jairus shows us the way to believe and hope in the face of the death of a loved one. Jesus restored to life only a few people during the days of His earthly ministry, but His resurrection testifies to His gift of His eternal presence with both the living and the dead in Christ. The professional mourners show us how not to seek to help bereaved people.

❖ Spiritual Transformations

Jairus came to Jesus asking that He come and save his dying daughter; Jesus went with him. On the way, messengers came to announce that the girl was dead and that Jesus need not come. Jesus, however, urged Jairus to continue to have faith. When they arrived at Jairus's house, Jesus cast out the professional mourners. Then He went in to the girl and called her back from death's clutches.

In this lesson we are focusing on how to minister to others when their loved one is sick, dying, or dead. In every case, prayer is the first step. Second, faith and love can be expressed by acts of compassion. We can give the gift of our presence and do what we can to help. When we are the ones hurting, we can accept the loving ministry of others. When others are hurting, we can act to help and comfort them in every way possible: visiting; bringing food; house-sitting during funerals; expressing words of comfort; and sending cards, letters, flowers or memorial gifts.

In what ways have you ministered to people whose loved ones were sick, dying, or dead? _____

In what other ways could you minister to them? _____

Prayer of Commitment: Lord, sustain us in the face of sickness, death, and bereavement, and help us be used to help others at such times. Amen.

[1]A. T. Robertson, *Word Pictures in the New Testament*, vol. 1 [Nashville: Broadman Press, 1930], 301.

[2]James A. Brooks, "Mark," in *The New American Commentary*, vol. 23 [Nashville: Broadman Press, 1991], 94.

[3]The Mishnah, Ketuboth 4.4.

[4]Herschel H. Hobbs, *An Exposition of the Gospel of Mark* [Grand Rapids: Baker Book House, 1970], 87-88.

MINISTRY IN NATURAL DISASTER

Background Passage: Acts 27:1–28:10
Focal Passage: Acts 27:14,20,22-25,33-36; 28:2,7-10
Key Verse: Acts 27:25

❖ *Significance of the Lesson*

• The *Theme* of this lesson is that during a natural disaster, Christians can rely on God's strength and help others trust Him.
• The *Life Question* addressed by this lesson is, How can I hold things together when the world seems to be falling apart?
• The *Biblical Truth* is that believers who rely on God's strength can help others trust Him during times of natural disaster.
• The *Life Impact* is to help you help others during times of natural disaster.

Natural Disasters

The images of natural disasters—floods, earthquakes, avalanches, fires, hurricanes, and tornadoes—have become commonplace because of the quick reporting on television. As a result, many adults are no longer moved by such images unless they pose a danger to them or to someone they care about. Some adults live in fear that a natural disaster will befall them or someone they love.

In the biblical worldview, storms and other natural disasters are part of this imperfect world. God gives believers the assurance of His love and care when they experience natural disasters, although He does not always deliver them from danger. He always wants Christians to trust in Him, to encourage others, and to minister to the needs of others in the midst of such disasters.

Paul's Trip to Rome

When Paul wrote a letter to the church at Rome, he told them that he wanted to visit Rome after he delivered the offering to Jerusalem

(Rom. 15:24-33). He did get to Rome—but not the way he had expected. When he was in Jerusalem, he was almost killed. The Romans arrested him. He had several hearings, and the Romans could not find he had committed any crime against Rome. Faced with even more trials and in danger of assassination, Paul exercised his right as a Roman citizen to appeal his case to Caesar. Acts 27:1–28:16 tells of his eventful trip to Rome. The long account of the storm at sea is still one of the ancient sources for navigation in that day. From the biblical point of view, we can learn from this account how believers are to respond to natural disasters.

Word Study: *No little kindness*

The Greek behind the words **no little kindness** in Acts 28:2 is *ou ten tuchousan philanthropian.* This phrase means literally "not the common kindness toward human beings." A. T. Robertson suggested the translation "not the kindness that happens everyday."[1] *Tuchousan,* translated **little,** means "usual" or "ordinary." When "not" is used with it, the meaning is "unusual" or "extraordinary." This is what is called a *litotes,* a negative statement that is used to make an affirmative statement. It is also an understatement that is used to increase the effect. This same word, *tuchousan,* is used with the negative in 19:11, which literally reads, "God performed miracles, *not the ones having commonly occurred,* by the hand of Paul." The *King James Version* translates this "God wrought *special* miracles by the hands of Paul." The *New Revised Standard Version* reads "God did *extraordinary* miracles through Paul" (italics added to show the translation of *tuchousan*). Such were the actions of the **barbarous people** in Acts 28:2, they demonstrated "extraordinary kindness" (NASB, HCSB). **Kindness** translates the word *philanthropia* (from which we get our word *philanthropy*). It combines the words for "love" and "man." This is a love or kindness toward fellow human beings.

❖ *Search the Scriptures*

The sudden storm that swept down on the ship carrying Paul to Rome posed a danger to all aboard. Paul testified of God's assurance to him that there would be no loss of life. He counseled them to eat in order to be prepared to survive the wreck of the ship. After the shipwreck, Paul ministered to the people of the island Malta; and they showed hospitality to Paul and the others.

If you have a map of Paul's journeys in your Bible, it would be good to consult it as you study this lesson.

Disaster Strikes (Acts 27:14,20)

How did Paul come to be on this ship? What kind of natural disaster threatened them? How serious was the threat? Did everyone—including the believers—give up hope of being saved? What lessons does this show us about the coming of disasters?

27:14: But not long after there arose against it a tempestuous wind, called Euroclydon.

From the early part of chapter 27 we learn that Paul and some other prisoners were assigned to a centurion named Julius. They embarked on a ship of Adramyttium [ad-ruh-MIT-ih-uhm], a seaport in Asia Minor. They changed to a ship bound for Rome when they got to Myra, on the southern coast of Asia Minor. Since the prevailing winds were from the west, it was hard going for the sailing vessel to reach Crete. They stopped in Fair Havens on the southern coast of the island. Then they debated whether to try to make Phoenix, a better harbor from which to face the storm season. Paul argued against going farther. The day of Atonement ("the fast") already had come. This Jewish fast day occurred in late September or early October. This was the beginning of the storm season for that part of the Mediterranean Sea. Paul knew that, and so did all on board. However, the centurion accepted the recommendation of the captain and owner of the ship that they press on.

At first all went well because there was a soft south wind. Then disaster struck. **Not long after** they began the voyage along the south side of Crete, **there arose against** the ship **a tempestuous wind, called Euroclydon** [yoo-RAHK-lih-dahn]. The word **tempestuous** translates *typhones*, from which we get the word *typhoon*. This was a storm with a strong circular motion. Such whirling winds are caused by the clash of opposing air masses. It was "a wind of hurricane force" (NIV). Sailors dreaded this wind so much that they had a name for it, the "Euraquilo" [yoo-RAHK-wih-luh] (NASB) or "northeaster" (NIV, NRSV, HCSB)—this is the word that is used in the oldest manuscripts of the Book of Acts. (The word used in the manuscripts the *King James Version* followed, **Euroclydon,** refers "to a southeast gale, but this is not the dreaded storm of the Mediterranean. The northeasterly storm *is*."[2])

For many years New Testament scholars thought that "Euraquilo" was a word found only here. However, an inscription has now been found with this word on it. The inscription is in a pavement that "contains a mosaic design depicting the winds in a twelve-point format. The Latin term *euraquilon* occurs in the position thirty degrees north of east. . . . The term seems to be a hybrid formed from the Greek *euros* (east wind) and Latin *aquilo* (north wind)."[3] The word thus means "The Northeaster" (CEV).

The sudden strong winds swept down from the northeast and drove the little ship away from the shelter of Crete out into the broad expanse of the Mediterranean Sea. The sailors were unable to maintain their course toward the northwest. Thus, instead of reaching the safe harbor of Phoenix, they were blown wherever the wind moved them.

27:20: And when neither sun nor stars in many days appeared, and no small tempest lay on us, all hope that we should be saved was then taken away.

The crew did what they could to survive. First, they secured "the lifeboat" (NIV) or "the skiff" (NKJV, HCSB; vv. 16-17a). This was a small boat towed behind the ship. It was interfering with the ship's progress and steering, and possibly it may have been in danger of being smashed against the side of the ship. It had to be taken on board. Then they undergirded the ship with "helps" (KJV) or "ropes" (NIV, HCSB). These cables were an attempt to keep the ship from being broken apart by the storm. Their third action is not completely clear. According to the *King James Version,* they set the mainsail ("strake sail," v. 17). "This is, however, most unlikely. Depending on how it was set with relation to the wind, this would either have driven them into the shoals they were trying to avoid or would have exposed the sails to the full violence of the wind and ripped them to shreds. It is more likely that they lowered the gear for the topsails and only set the small storm sail, allowing the ship to drift. A third possibility is that they lowered a drift anchor from the stern that would drag in the water and slow their progress" toward the dreaded sandbars off the coast of North Africa.[4] This is the view represented in the *New International Version*'s rendering of verse 17b—"they lowered the sea anchor and let the ship be driven along." Fourth, they threw their cargo overboard to lighten their load (v. 18). Their fifth recorded action was to do the same with the ship's tackle—possibly "the long spar used to support the mainsail"—the next day (v. 19).[5]

Days passed and they saw **neither sun nor stars.** This was before the use of the compass, and ships navigated by the sun and stars. Being unable to see these, they had no idea where they were. **No small tempest lay on us** is another *litotes* in which a negative statement is used to make an affirmative statement and an understatement increases the effect. The *New International Version* brings out this positive and increased meaning—"the storm continued raging"—as does the *Holman Christian Standard Bible*—"the severe storm kept raging." As a result, Luke wrote, **All hope that we should be saved was then taken away. Saved** and **hope** are used here not of Christian hope and salvation but of hope of deliverance from the storm—"Our last hopes of coming through alive began to fade" (NEB, REB).

Acts 27 is one of the so-called "we-passages" in the Book of Acts. These were the times when Luke was present in the action being described. Another friend of Paul's, Aristarchus [ehr-iss-TAHR-kuhs] (v. 2), was also aboard. All totaled, there were 276 people on board (v. 37). Among these were Julius and some Roman soldiers, the crew, the prisoners, and other passengers. Despair seems to have settled on all of them—at least for the time being. We don't know whether Paul felt this despair, but we are told that he was praying and later shared with the others what he had learned from the Lord. For the time being despair gripped those aboard the hapless ship.

So far, we have learned these facts. (1) Human beings have always lived in a world of earthquakes, famines, and other troubles. (2) Natural disasters often are sudden and unexpected, even when they happen under conditions conducive to them. (3) Fear and despair are normal human reactions to severe natural disasters.

Encouragement Given (Acts 27:22-25)

What did Paul promise? How was this different from his earlier prediction? What was the basis for his encouraging words?

27:22-25: And now I exhort you to be of good cheer: for there shall be no loss of any man's life among you, but of the ship. ²³For there stood by me this night the angel of God, whose I am, and whom I serve, ²⁴saying, Fear not, Paul; thou must be brought before Caesar: and, lo, God hath given thee all them that sail with thee. ²⁵Wherefore, sirs, be of good cheer: for I believe God, that it shall be even as it was told me.

Fear and despair are normal human reactions to such terrible disasters when we find ourselves in them. We should do all we can to enable ourselves and others to survive. Yet in such storms, even believers may have their faith shaken. R. B. Rackham believed that even Paul initially felt the sense of despair but quickly moved through this to pray for himself and others: "In this situation their first need was encouragement, and St. Paul, the great apostle of 'comfort,' was enabled to encourage them, as he had so often encouraged the disciples. But first he had himself to experience the depression and fear. It was small satisfaction for his prediction to have been verified, if this was to be the end of all—instead of Rome, a watery grave."[6]

When Paul arose to speak to the others (v. 21), he could not resist reminding them that he had told them this would happen (v. 10). Yet he changed one important part of his earlier prediction in verse 10. He had warned that lives would be lost. Now he exhorted them **to be of good cheer** and assured them **there shall be no loss of any man's life among you, but of the ship.**

Paul explained how he knew this. Paul said that the assurance came from **God, whose I am, and whom I serve.** The message came through **the angel of God.** The messenger had **stood by** Paul on that **night.** The message contained a twofold assurance. First, the angel told Paul, **Thou must be brought before Caesar.** Second, he was promised, **God hath given thee all them that sail with thee. Given** translates the verb form of *charis,* the word for *grace.* Thus it may be translated "God has graciously given" (NIV, HCSB). This wording implies that Paul had been praying not only for his own deliverance but also for all who were on board. Now he encouraged them a second time to **be of good cheer,** and then added, **for I believe God, that it shall be even as it was told me.**

This was not Paul's first time to face shipwreck. Earlier he had written of being shipwrecked three times, having spent one day and one night awaiting rescue (2 Cor. 11:25). Therefore, he knew that God can deliver *from* a storm, and He can also deliver *through* a storm. Sometimes He stops a storm; at other times, He is with us as we live through the storm. When a tornado swept through our city a few years ago, one man saw the black cloud almost upon him. He got out of his car and ran toward a building, where he expected to be safe. Suddenly someone tackled him from behind and threw his weight on him. The stranger continued to lie on him until the wind calmed.

The stranger got up and slipped away before the man could get to his feet. Then the man saw that the building toward which he had been running was in ruins. If the stranger had not held him down, he figured he would have been killed. That man believes the Lord sent some kind of angel to save him.

Nowhere in Acts 27 is it stated that God sent the storm. It was the kind of natural disaster that grew out of natural forces at work. However, when the storm took place, Paul found help and assurance from the Lord. We seldom know why disasters happen, but we always know that God can work in evil circumstances to bring good out of evil.

Being in natural disasters should always remind us of our need for God. Being in one of these disasters also should make us sensitive to others in such times. First, Paul knew that drawing strength from the Lord's presence at such times was important. He also knew that it was appropriate to be concerned for the welfare of others. When we find ourselves in such situations, we should follow Paul's example of faith and concern. Second, Paul knew that during such times people need encouragement. Twice he told them **be of good cheer.** The rest of Paul's verbal message that God was going to spare all of their lives was likewise a word of great encouragement.

From verses 22-25 we learn these principles: (1) Discovering God's presence in the midst of storms and listening to His message is important. (2) In the midst of storms our concerns should include others and not merely be for ourselves. (3) We should believe that God can meet our most desperate needs in the midst of the storms. (4) We should believe that God can deliver out of the storms both those who know Him and those who do not. (5) We should trust that His will is best. (6) Those who know God are in a position to encourage others with a word from the Lord, and they should do so.

Physical Needs Attended (Acts 27:33-36)

When did Paul urge those on the ship to eat? Why did he do this? How did he do this?

27:33-36: And while the day was coming on, Paul besought them all to take meat, saying, This day is the fourteenth day that ye have tarried and continued fasting, having taken nothing. [34]Wherefore I pray you to take some meat: for this is for your health: for there shall not an hair fall from the head of any of you. [35]And when

he had thus spoken, he took bread, and gave thanks to God in presence of them all: and when he had broken it, he began to eat. [36]Then were they all of good cheer, and they also took some meat.

Acts 27 contains several time references. "The third day" is mentioned in verse 19. Verse 27 mentions "the fourteenth night." On that night the sailors sensed that the ship was approaching land. Depth soundings showed that they were right: "They dropped four anchors from the stern and prayed for daylight" (v. 29, NIV). Then the frantic crew tried to save themselves in the lifeboat. Paul warned the centurion, and this desertion was thwarted. The soldiers cut the lines to the lifeboat to prevent a further attempt.

Then, **While the day was coming on** ("just before dawn," NIV), **Paul besought them all to take meat** ("urged them all to eat," NIV). Although he reassured them that "Not one of you will lose a single hair from his head" (NIV), Paul knew that all would need their strength to survive. Paul said, **This is for your health** ("You need it to survive," NIV). Literally, he said, "This is for the necessity of your salvation." The word translated **health** is the word for "salvation" or "deliverance" (*soterias*). In this context it means deliverance from the storm. However, Paul's use of this word may also imply the need for spiritual salvation, which would be impossible for unbelievers if they perished.

Paul set the example: **He took bread, and gave thanks to God in presence of them all.** This was a testimony of his gratitude to and confidence in God. It also encouraged the others to follow his example. We are not told whether all gave thanks to God, but they all took courage and ate.

Victims and survivors of natural disasters have need of encouragement, but they also have physical needs for food, and often for water, shelter, and clothes. One of the most practical and needed ministries to victims of serious disasters—natural or manmade—is physical aid. Mission boards, state conventions, and individual churches often undertake such ministries.

From verses 33-36 we learn these principles: (1) Victims of disasters need encouragement, but they also need food and to have other physical needs met. (2) Christians can provide for such needs, whether individually, collectively, or cooperatively. (3) Helping to provide for others' physical needs in the midst of disasters should be done with gratitude to God.

Kindness Shown (Acts 28:2,7-10)

How did the people of Malta show kindness to Paul and the other survivors of the shipwreck? How did Paul show kindness to them?
28:2: And the barbarous people showed us no little kindness: for they kindled a fire, and received us everyone, because of the present rain, and because of the cold.

Much happened between Acts 27:36 and 28:2. After the 276 people had eaten, they threw overboard the rest of the grain in an attempt to lighten the ship. They hoped not to run aground. As they neared land, the soldiers wanted to kill the prisoners lest they escape; however, once again Julius saved Paul's life. They spotted "a certain creek with a shore" ("a bay with a sandy beach," NIV) and steered toward it, but soon ran upon a sandbar and became stuck. Then the waves began to break up the ship. Everyone made it to shore alive as Paul had predicted.

However, when those from the ship came out of the sea, they found a **cold** and rainy day. But they also found a roaring **fire.** The fire was the work of the people of the island on which they had landed. **Melita** [MEL-ih-tuh] is the name for what we call Malta. The Greeks referred to all foreigners as **barbarous people** or *barbarians.* Their word was *barbaroi.* The word came from the notion to the Greeks that the words of all who did not speak Greek sounded like "bar-bar-bar."

Notice how these non-Christian people responded to the 276 strangers suddenly thrown up on their small island. Paul wrote that they **showed us no little kindness.** As explained in the "Word Study," this expression is a *litotes* in which a negative statement is used to make an affirmative statement and an understatement increases the effect. What the islanders did was to show the shipwreck victims "unusual" (NIV) or "extraordinary" (NASB) kindness. If such non-Christians showed such kindness to strangers, how much more should Christians demonstrate their love and kindness to others? Not only had **they kindled a fire** for the wet and cold survivors, but they **received us everyone. Received** translates the same word Paul used in Romans 14:3 and 15:7 to describe how Christ receives sinners and how Christians are to welcome one another—in spite of differences of opinion.

After surviving the shipwreck, verses 3-6 describe how a poisonous snake came out from by the fire and bit Paul. Initially this led the people to think that Paul was a murderer. But the bite failed to harm him, and this led the people to change their minds—now they thought Paul was a god!

28:7-10: In the same quarters were possessions of the chief man of the island, whose name was Publius; who received us, and lodged us three days courteously. [8]And it came to pass, that the father of Publius lay sick of a fever and of a bloody flux: to whom Paul entered in, and prayed, and laid his hands on him, and healed him. [9]So when this was done, others also, which had diseases in the island, came, and were healed: [10]who also honored us with many honors; and when we departed, they laded us with such things as were necessary.

Paul and his companions were welcomed into the home **of the chief man of the island, whose name was Publius** [PUHB-lih-uhs]. Luke wrote that **Publius** not only **received us,** but that he **lodged us three days courteously. Lodged** is a word that means "to welcome strangers." It is used in Hebrews 13:2 of Abraham, who "entertained angels unawares." **Courteously** means "in a friendly manner" or "with hospitality." Surely Christians should be as hospitable in times of disaster as this man was.

At the same time, **Publius** had his own problems with disaster: **The father of Publius lay sick of a fever and of a bloody flux.** In other words, he had a fever and "dysentery" (NIV, HCSB, NKJV, NRSV). Paul found a practical way to express gratitude and show kindness to Publius by healing his father. When the people of Malta heard of this, they brought other sick and diseased people, and they **were healed.** Two different words for healing are found in verses 8 and 9. Some Bible students think that *iasato* (v. 8) refers to a miraculous healing by Paul, but that *etherapeuonto* (from which we get our word *therapy*) in verse 9 may refer to some medical work by Luke the physician. Those who believe this interpret the words **honored** and **honors** as fees for medical services (as in our word *honorarium*). The Greek word, however, regularly refers to "signs of respect," and that fits better in this passage that stresses the hospitality of the people of Malta rather than indicating that they paid Luke for practicing medicine.

Not only did the people of Malta honor them with many honors, but **when** they **departed,** the Maltese also provided all the supplies the travelers would need as they continued their voyage to Rome: **They laded us with such things as were necessary** ("they furnished us with the supplies we needed," NIV).

Both the Maltese people and Paul and his companions showed kindness toward one another. The people welcomed and cared for the shivering survivors of the storm and shipwreck. Later they honored their guests and sent them on their way with adequate provisions. Paul healed Publius's father and the sick who were brought to him.

From 28:2,7-10 we learn these principles: (1) If non-Christians can show kindness to fellow human beings, how much more should Christians? (2) Christians have unique power and opportunities to show kindnesses to others in ways people of the world cannot. We should never forget this as we minister to both body and soul.

❖ *Spiritual Transformations*

A sudden, violent storm swept down on the ship carrying Paul to Rome. Those on board did all they could, but still the storm continued. All felt that they had no hope of surviving the storm. Paul encouraged his fellow passengers by saying that God had assured him that no lives would be lost. Paul encouraged the weary people to eat some food so they would have strength for what lay ahead. When they shipwrecked on Malta, the local leader and people of Malta showed kindness to Paul and the other survivors. Paul and his companions showed kindness to them by healing their sick.

When we have an opportunity to minister to people who are victims of natural disasters, we can encourage them, provide for their physical and spiritual needs, and show them every kind of kindness within our power.

What has been your personal experience with natural disasters?

_____

What are some of the ways in which you can help victims of natural disasters? _____

Prayer of Commitment: Lord, guide us to help people who are victims of natural disasters. Amen.

[1]A. T. Robertson, *Word Pictures in the New Testament*, vol. 3 [Nashville: Broadman Press, 1930], 477.

[2]John B. Polhill, "Acts," in *The New American Commentary*, vol. 26 [Nashville: Broadman Press, 1992], 520. The italics is the author's.

[3]Polhill, "Acts," NAC, 520.

[4]Polhill, "Acts," NAC, 521.

[5]Polhill, "Acts," NAC, 522.

[6]R. B. Rackham, *The Acts of the Apostles*, 14th ed., in the Westminster Commentaries [London: Methuen & Co. Ltd., 1953], 486.

MINISTRY IN TIMES OF CONFLICT

Background Passage: 1 Corinthians 1:10-17; 3:1-23
Focal Passage: 1 Corinthians 1:10; 3:3-17
Key Verse: 1 Corinthians 1:10

❖ *Significance of the Lesson*

• The *Theme* of this lesson is that when people or churches are in conflict, Christians can help build unity.
• The *Life Question* addressed in this lesson is, How can I help build unity when conflict arises in my church?
• The *Biblical Truth* is that Christ desires unity in the church.
• The *Life Impact* is to help you build unity in your church.

Worldviews About Conflict

In the secular worldview, conflict is considered normal. Conflict can be found everywhere—between nations, within a nation, between neighbors, at work, in families, and even within churches.

In the biblical worldview, believers are united by their common relationship with Jesus Christ. Petty differences should not produce dissension and strife. No group of people will always agree on every issue, but Christians can work together for unity by agreeing on what is important and building on that. Jesus Christ is most important.

Paul and the Corinthian Church

Paul had a stormy relation with the Corinthian church. He was the missionary who first brought the good news to Corinth (Acts 18:1-17). This was on Paul's second missionary journey. Much of his third journey was spent in Ephesus (Acts 19–20). While he was in Ephesus (1 Cor. 16:8), he received a letter from the Corinthians asking him several questions (7:1). He also had visitors from Corinth who told him of problems and issues in the Corinthian church (1:11). We learn from 1 Corinthians 5:9-11 that Paul already had directed them not to form compromising relations with unbelievers. Paul wrote 1 Corinthians to deal with their questions and problems. Within the letter are some strong hints that all was not well between the church and the apostle (see chap. 4).

Between the writing of 1 and 2 Corinthians the church situation deteriorated even further. Paul made a painful visit and wrote a harsh letter to the congregation (2 Cor. 2:1-4). By the time he wrote 2 Corinthians, some degree of reconciliation had been achieved there. The church had repudiated a ringleader who was opposing Paul (2:5-11).

Thus we learn that there was a group within the church who were opposed to Paul. They questioned his claim to be an apostle. They were critical of his preaching and leadership. They considered themselves more spiritual and wiser than Paul. They were already at work when Paul wrote 1 Corinthians, but later they temporarily gained the support of the majority in the church. This spirit of opposition lies behind both of Paul's letters to the Corinthians.

Word Study: *Divisions*

Schismata is a key word in 1 Corinthians. We get our word *schism* from it. It means either "divisions" or "dissensions." The word was used to depict a tear in an old garment (Mark 2:21). In 1 Corinthians it was used not only in 1:10 but also in 11:18 of different groups at the Lord's Supper and in 12:25 for discord in the church body. Although most English translations use the word "divisions," these divisions had not yet resulted in different groups going their own way. They were still in one church, but the church was filled with a spirit of dissension. Perhaps the word "factions" would describe their situation.

❖ *Search the Scriptures*

Paul urged the Corinthians to turn aside from dissensions and to come to oneness of spirit. He accused them of acting like non-Christians when they showed envy and strife. He explained that human leaders in a church were only servants of the Lord. The Lord owned the church and did its work. Paul spoke of his own work in Corinth as laying a foundation, and he called on others to build worthy buildings on the foundation. He delivered a serious warning to those who would destroy the church.

Appeal for Unity (1 Cor. 1:10)

How did Paul use the word **same** *in this verse? What were the* **divisions** *against which he warned?*

1:10: Now I beseech you, brethren, by the name of our Lord Jesus Christ, that ye all speak the same thing, and that there be no divisions among you; but that ye be perfectly joined together in the same mind and in the same judgment.

Although Paul was about to deal with some serious problems in the church, he began with words of commendation and gratitude (1:4-9). He referred to his readers as **brethren.** He was not about to accuse them of being non-Christians, although he would tell them they were acting that way. Some visitors from Corinth had brought Paul bad news. The church was arguing over human leaders. Four groups were supporting each of the following: Paul, Apollos, Cephas (Peter), and Christ. The issues seemed to have been more about the style of leadership than the content of doctrine. We don't know much about the Christ party, but they were probably the ones who claimed greater spirituality than the rest of the church.

The differences of opinion between the four groups had become divisive. They had not divided into four churches, but there were four distinct groups within one church. Paul strongly condemned such factions.

Paul used the Greek word for **same** three times in verse 10. He called on them all to **speak the same thing.** The problem was that they were saying different things in their idolatrous loyalty to one leader. What people say often lights the fires of dissension, which lead to factions and sometimes to separation.

Then he urged them to **be perfectly joined together in the same mind and in the same judgment** ("be united with the same understanding and the same conviction," HCSB). He was not calling for uniformity but for unity with appropriate diversity. When Christians have the same basic convictions and speak the same basic testimony, this makes for unity.

Be perfectly joined together, or "be perfectly united" (NIV), is *katertismenoi,* a word that refers to returning something to its right condition. It was used of mending nets (Matt 4:21). The normal condition of a church is to have oneness of spirit based on common love for Christ and for one another. **In the same mind and in the same judgment** does not refer to absolute agreement about every subject and issue. But it does call for the same kind of devotion to the Lord that binds together different kinds of people into one body of Christ.

From Paul's appeal in verse 10, we see (1) that dissension in a church can lead to factions and divisions and (2) that a church should have a unity without uniformity.

Disunity: Evidence of Worldliness (1 Cor. 3:3-4)

*What is the meaning of **carnal**? Why is the word **I** a key to the cause of the disunity? What is the meaning of the word translated **strife**? What other kinds of dissensions are reflected in 1 Corinthians?*

3:3-4: For ye are yet carnal: for whereas there is among you envying, and strife, and divisions, are ye not carnal, and walk as men? ⁴For while one saith, I am of Paul; and another, I am of Apollos; are ye not carnal?

To understand these verses, read 2:14–3:2. Paul used four different words to describe different kinds of people. The "spiritual" person (*pneumatikos*) is the person whose life is surrendered to and led by the Spirit of God. The "natural man" (*psychikos*) is someone who lives without any experience with the Spirit. Two different Greek words are translated **carnal** in verses 1 and 3 (*sarkinos* and *sarkikos*, respectively). Some Greek scholars think that the two words have basically the same meaning; others make a distinction. Those who see a difference think the word in verse 1 involves a less serious condition than that described by the word in verse 3.

The charge in verses 1-2 is spiritual immaturity. The charge in verse 3 is living like non-Christians, or what Paul also called living according to the flesh. He did not accuse his readers of being non-Christians; he accused them of living like those who do not believe.

Both warnings are in order. Verses 1-2 call us to avoid spiritual immaturity. The symptoms of this include being babies in Christ long after our conversion. This condition is caused by a failure to mature in Christ. Verses 3-4 warn that some professing Christians can act like non-Christians. Paul specifically referred to **envying** (*zelos*)—or "jealousy" (NIV, NASB, NRSV)—and **strife** (*eris*). *Eris* was the name given by the Greeks to the goddess of war. Herodotus used this word to describe political and domestic strife. In Romans 13:13 *zelos* and *eris* are listed with the sins of a sensual way of life. The situation in churches that have jealously and strife resembles a bar-room brawl. The words *church* and *fight* ought not be found together.

At the heart of the problem of **divisions** or dissension is the sin of selfish pride. Notice that the supporters of each leader claimed,

I am of (compare 1:12). "It was as if a man said, 'Look at me. *I* belong to Paul.' The emphasis was on *I*, not on Paul. This self-assertive spirit was the cause of the dissension and strife. When this kind of selfishness is at work, any issue can become the storm center of strife. Take the issue in Corinth, for example: who I support is actually much less important than the fact that *I* support him. Once committed to a position, selfish pride demands that *I* remain adamant. My leader is bound to be the best; after all, don't *I* support him?"[1]

A study of 1 Corinthians reveals that arguing about leaders was only one of several areas of destructive dissension in the church. Some of these believers had legal disputes against one another (6:1-8). They also were divided on the issue of whether to eat meat sacrificed to idols (chaps. 8–10). The role of women in church worship was another debate (11:1-16). The Lord's Supper was a topic about which one group mistreated another (vv. 17-34). Spiritual gifts, especially speaking in tongues, were proving to be divisive (chaps. 12–14). Each of these divisions grew out of selfish pride.

Some of these are still issues that lead churches down the same road that was taken by the Corinthians. Differences in opinions about and loyalties to leaders are often the occasion for factions to develop. One of the issues in our day is the style of worship, especially the style of music used. Arguments about money and church property can become caustic. Strong differences of opinion on almost any issue can become divisive if selfish pride rules in the hearts of members.

Dissension in the Corinthian church was a serious problem. Achieving unity after conflict has arisen is not easy. It is better for a church to be constantly on guard against anything that might lead to destructive dissension. For we know that Christians are to "keep the unity of the Spirit in the bond of peace" (Eph. 4:3), and we know that disunity in the church is evidence of worldliness.

From verses 3-4 we learned that (1) jealousy and strife in a church produce behavior like that of non-Christians and that (2) arguing over leaders is not only idolatrous but also evidence of selfish pride.

Role of Leaders (1 Cor. 3:5-9)

What do these verses teach about church work? Who owns the church? Who grows the church? What should be the relationship between church leaders?

3:5-9: **Who then is Paul, and who is Apollos, but ministers by whom ye believed, even as the Lord gave to every man? [6]I have planted, Apollos watered; but God gave the increase. [7]So then neither is he that planteth anything, neither he that watereth; but God that giveth the increase. [8]Now he that planteth and he that watereth are one: and every man shall receive his own reward according to his own labor. [9]For we are laborers together with God: ye are God's husbandry, ye are God's building.**

Paul used himself and **Apollos** as examples. Immature leaders would be flattered by the kind of loyalty given to these men by some partisan supporters, but mature leaders such as Paul and Apollos were not pleased by such idolatrous support. We may wonder why Paul dealt only with himself and Apollos, leaving out Peter (Cephas; see 1:12). Probably the main differences were between the supporters of these two. Apollos was younger and more eloquent than Paul (see Acts 18:24-26). He went to Corinth soon after Paul left (vv. 27-28; 19:1). Those who did not like Paul easily formed a vocal preference for Apollos, without any support for this from Apollos.

Paul and Apollos had no jealousy toward each other. Paul simply used Apollos as an example (1 Cor. 4:6). When Paul closed this letter, he urged the church to welcome Apollos (16:12). Later Paul told Titus to help Apollos on one of his journeys (Titus 3:13).

In counteracting the idolatrous loyalty of the supporters of each, Paul asked, **Who** ("what," NIV, HCSB) **then is Paul, and who** ("what," NIV, HCSB) **is Apollos?** Paul said that they were **ministers** or "servants" (NIV, HCSB) of God and of the people. Leaders who follow the biblical model are servant-leaders. Being a servant is an exalted privilege in the New Testament. Jesus was the Servant who came not to be served but to serve, and He called His followers also to be servants. Paul and Apollos were not gods but servants.

About whom was Paul writing when he wrote **even as the Lord gave to every man**? Some Bible students believe Paul was thinking of the believers whom he had just mentioned. More likely, he had in mind the leaders to whom God gave different gifts and tasks. They were part of **one** work and purpose, but **every man shall receive his own reward according to his own labor.** Leaders come and go, but the Lord's work goes on.

Using the analogy of agriculture, Paul wrote, **I have planted, Apollos watered; but God gave the increase.** The two leaders were only workers on the farm. Each had his part of the task. Paul was the one who first brought the gospel to Corinth. He sowed the seed. Apollos followed him and watered the field. But the key words are **God gave the increase.** The church belongs to the Lord, not to the leaders or to the members. The work of growing a church is God's work; He uses human leaders in His work; however, it is His work. Only He can cause the seed to grow and mature. The emphasis should be on God's work, not on the workers. The one who plants and the one who waters are nothing as compared to God, who causes the crop to grow.

Verse 9 can be translated in two ways. The translation found in the *King James Version* emphasizes that we are working together in tandem with God: **We are laborers together with God** (similarly NEB, NASB, NIV, HCSB). The emphasis in the translation found in the *New Revised Standard Version* is on the mutual work of Paul and Apollos, both in service to God: "We are God's servants, working together" (similarly REB). Two things are clear: this is God's work, and He entrusts His work to servants whom He calls to do specific tasks.

How many church fights have been the result of people stating preferences for one pastor over another? We need to realize that pastors come and go. Each has distinctive gifts, and God sends each to a church for a special need. But church leaders are servants, and they have different tasks to accomplish in God's plan.

Paul had been comparing the church to **God's husbandry** ("God's field," NIV, HCSB), and he was about to compare it to **God's building.** In Greek, the first word in the verse is **God.** Literally, it reads, "God's fellowworkers we are; God's field, God's building you are." What a contrast to the verses beginning with **I.** When God is first, all is as it should be; when I am first, all goes wrong.

From verses 5-9 we learn: (1) The church is God's work, but He calls servant-leaders to be used in His work. (2) Servant-leaders do their part, and God uses all of them to do His work.

Foundation of Unity (1 Cor. 3:10-15)

What do these verses teach about building the church? In what sense was Paul a wise masterbuilder? Why is Christ the only foundation? Who were the ones building on the foundation? What did the fire represent?

3:10-15: According to the grace of God which is given unto me, as a wise masterbuilder, I have laid the foundation, and another

buildeth thereon. But let every man take heed how he buildeth thereupon. [11]For other foundation can no man lay than that is laid, which is Jesus Christ. [12]Now if any man build upon this foundation gold, silver, precious stones, wood, hay, stubble; [13]every man's work shall be made manifest: for the day shall declare it, because it shall be revealed by fire; and the fire shall try every man's work of what sort it is. [14]If any man's work abide which he hath built thereupon, he shall receive a reward. [15]If any man's work shall be burned, he shall suffer loss: but he himself shall be saved; yet so as by fire.

The work Paul had been given by God was **according to the grace of God.** Paul knew that whatever work he did was the work of God's grace and power in and through him. Paul was not too timid to point out that he was used by God to bring the good news to Corinth first. He had planted the seed; he was the **wise masterbuilder.** He had **laid the foundation** of the church. However, all of this was made possible by the grace of God. Paul was not the foundation. He laid the only true and lasting foundation for the church, **which is Jesus Christ.**

Paul's ministry was primarily to start the church by laying this foundation. Those who followed him built on that foundation. Some built well with materials comparable to **gold, silver,** and **precious stones.** Others built poorly with inferior materials comparable to **wood, hay,** and **stubble.** Who were those who built on the sure foundation? Leon Morris wrote: "Some restrict the application of this passage to the work of teachers. But the words seem capable of more general application. While it is especially true of teachers, it is also true in a measure of every believer that he is engaged in building on the one foundation. Let him take heed how he builds!"[2]

In church work each of us is building on the same solid foundation. We also are building on the work of those who have gone before us. The quality of our work will eventually be judged and tested. Those who built worthily on the foundation will find that what they built lasts. Those who built shacks on this magnificent foundation will find them burned away. Verse 13 seems to refer to **the day** of judgment. Several words describe what will be done to what we have built: **made manifest . . . declare . . . revealed . . . try.** These words show that the quality of what we have built will be fully disclosed, and it will be tested **by fire.** Buildings made from cheap, flammable materials will be burned. The others will survive. The foundation will stand in either case. However, those who **suffer** the **loss** of that which they built will come through the experience like someone who escaped from a fire with only his life: **he himself shall be saved; yet so as by fire.** None of us should settle for entering heaven like someone with nothing to show for his or her living. Those who build unworthy lives or an unworthy ministry on the sure foundation will regret it.

From verses 10-15 we learn (1) that in the church and in the Christian life each of us builds on the foundation of Jesus Christ. (2) The quality of what we build will be tested, and we will either be rewarded or will suffer loss.

Seriousness of Disunity (1 Cor. 3:16-17)

What is the role of the Holy Spirit in the church? How do these verses compare with 1 Corinthians 6:19-20? How do people destroy the church? How will God destroy those who destroy the church?

3:16-17: Know ye not that ye are the temple of God, that the Spirit of God dwelleth in you? [17]**If any man defile the temple of God, him shall God destroy; for the temple of God is holy, which temple ye are.**

The church is not only a building; it is a special kind of building: **Ye are the temple of God.** The word for **temple** is *naos.* This word refers to the inner sanctuary of the temple, where God's presence dwelt in a special way. Paul explained, **The Spirit of God dwelleth in you.** The church as a whole is a temple in which the Spirit dwells. Paul's point in 3:16-17 is the danger of defiling and even destroying the church. **Defile** is *phtheirei,* the same word translated **destroy.** The word means to "destroy," "ruin," "corrupt," or "deprave."

Verses 16-17 contain a strong warning against destroying the church. Paul did not explain exactly what he meant either for humans to destroy the church or for God to destroy the destroyers. He may have been speaking of eternal punishment, which assumes that anyone who would destroy the temple of God's Spirit could not be a true child of God. Or, it may be that God would destroy a believer through earthly punishments. But surely no one would want to find out what Paul meant by daring to destroy a church!

Whatever Paul had in mind, it seems to have been more than what was described in verses 10-15, for the warning there was about building with inferior building materials on the foundation. That is serious enough, but Paul left no doubt that destroying a church is more deadly. Gordon D. Fee wrote: "This threat takes the warning of vv. 10-15 to its next step. The whole is addressed to the church. If a distinction is to be made between the 'anyone' of this passage and that of vv. 10-15, it would be that the focus here is more specifically on those few who seem to be the prime movers of the present quarrelings."[3] Those who continue to foster division in a church often will destroy it as a church.

From verses 16-17 we learn that (1) the church is the temple of the Holy Spirit, and (2) God will destroy anyone who destroys this temple.

❖ *Spiritual Transformations*

Paul tried to counteract factions in the Corinthian church by calling for common convictions and ways of speaking to one another. He said that churches filled with jealousy and strife are acting like non-Christians. Using himself and Apollos as examples, Paul showed how God used both servant-leaders to do His work. He compared the church to a field, a building, and a temple. Paul had laid the foundation of Christ, and each person built on that foundation. God will destroy those who destroy the church.

The "Life Impact" is to help you build unity in your church. This means that you must avoid any of the sins that lead to dissension and factions. You also will seek to stop any movement in that direction. You will be a peacemaker in tense situations. You will maintain good relations with your brothers and sisters in Christ, taking the initiative to be reconciled to anyone with a grudge toward you and anyone against whom you bear a grudge. You will support and pray for your pastor and other church leaders. And you will do nothing destructive to that local church.

What has been your experience and observation about churches that have divisive dissension? _____

What specific things can you do to enrich the spiritual oneness of your church? _____

Prayer of Commitment: Lord, help me to be a peacemaker, not a troublemaker, in Your church. Amen.

[1]Robert J. Dean, *First Corinthians for Today* [Nashville: Broadman Press, 1972], 32.
[2]Leon Morris, *The First Epistle of Paul to the Corinthians*, in the Tyndale New Testament Commentaries [Grand Rapids: William B. Eerdmans Publishing Company, 1958], 67.
[3]Gordon D. Fee, *The First Epistle to the Corinthians*, in the New International Commentary on the New Testament [Grand Rapids: William B. Eerdmans Publishing Company, 1987], 148.

MINISTRY TO PERSECUTED BELIEVERS

Background Passage: Acts 12:1-19
Focal Passage: Acts 12:1-17
Key Verse: Acts 12:5

❖ *Significance of the Lesson*

• The *Theme* of this lesson is that all Christians should be prepared to respond to persecution.

• The *Life Question* this lesson addresses is, How do I respond to persecution of Christians?

• The *Biblical Truth* is that believers are to pray for persecuted Christians while affirming that persecution cannot defeat God's purposes.

• The *Life Impact* is to help you be an advocate for persecuted Christians.

Persecution in Today's World

In the secular worldview, many people are not committed enough to any cause to suffer for it. Because they see little value in religion, they do not understand why anyone would be willing to suffer for it. Many adults are unaware of the fact that large-scale persecutions take place in today's world. Even those who champion human rights fail to see religious freedom as crucial to all freedoms.

The biblical worldview affirms that persecution of God's people is to be expected, but it cannot defeat God's purposes. Some believers know persecution firsthand. American Christians know about past persecutions, but they often know little of what is happening to believers in other lands today. As they become aware, they can respond to the Bible's call for prayer and action on behalf of their persecuted brothers and sisters.

King Herod

Four generations of the Herodian family are referred to in the New Testament. Four Herodians were rulers, and all four rejected Jesus

Christ—three of them with acts of violence. Herod the Great reigned with Roman permission over most of the land of Israel when Jesus was born. One of his final acts before his death in 4 B.C. was to kill the boy babies of Bethlehem (Matt. 2). He had many sons, some of whom he executed because he suspected them of plotting against him. At his death his kingdom was divided among his surviving sons. The most well-known of these was Herod Antipas, who was named tetrarch of Galilee and Perea. He beheaded John the Baptist (Matt. 14:1-12) and mocked Jesus (Luke 23:6-12). The Herod of Acts 12 was the grandson of Herod the Great, whose father Aristobulus [uh-riss-toh-BYOO-luhs] was executed by his grandfather. He was called Herod Agrippa I. He had a son also called Herod Agrippa II. He is the one to whom Paul preached in Acts 26.

Herod Agrippa I was sent to Rome as a child. He grew up with two of the future Caesars—Caligula and Claudius. Each of these rewarded him with land until he was king over much of his grandfather's realm. He—like the other Herods—served at the permission of the Romans. The Jewish historian Josephus told us that when in Rome Agrippa lived like the Romans did. However, Agrippa put on a show of piety when he was back in the land of the Jews. He tried to keep the Jews and the Romans pleased. This helps to explain his actions in Acts 12.

Word Study: *Vex*

The word *kakoo,* used in verse 1 of our Focal Passage, usually means to "harm" or "mistreat." It was used by Stephen to describe the oppression of Israel in Egypt (Acts 7:6,19). God used this word in His assurance that no one would harm Paul while he was in Corinth as a missionary (18:10). Peter used it to refer to the harm that comes to those who do wrong (1 Pet. 3:13). Of Herod Agrippa's actions in Acts 12:1, it is translated in a number of ways: "persecute" (NIV), "harass" (NKJV), "mistreat" (NASB), "attacked" (HCSB).

❖ *Search the Scriptures*

Herod Agrippa executed the apostle James and imprisoned Peter, planning to put him on trial. The church earnestly prayed for Peter. The angel of the Lord delivered Peter from prison. When Peter showed up where believers were praying for him, they at first didn't believe it was Peter. When they recognized him, he told them to tell James, the half brother of Jesus, about this event. Then Peter left Jerusalem.

Persecution (Acts 12:1-4)

Why did Herod launch a persecution of Christians? Why did he concentrate on leaders? How was the apostle James killed? What did Herod intend for Peter? What insights do these verses give us about persecution in our own day?

Verses 1-4: Now about that time Herod the king stretched forth his hands to vex certain of the church. [2]And he killed James the brother of John with the sword. [3]And because he saw it pleased the Jews, he proceeded further to take Peter also. (Then were the days of unleavened bread.) [4]And when he had apprehended him, he put him in prison, and delivered him to four quaternions of soldiers to keep him; intending after Easter to bring him forth to the people.

About that time referred to the time when Barnabas and Saul were in Jerusalem delivering the aid from the church at Antioch (see 11:30). Since Herod Agrippa was king from A.D. 37–44, the events of verses 1-17 were sometime within those years. Since Agrippa's death is recorded in 12:20-23, the persecution of verses 1-17 probably took place late in his reign. The Jerusalem church already had been through two waves of persecution. The first of these was instigated by the Sadducees, who were upset by the preaching of the apostles that the Sadducees had crucified Jesus and God had raised Him from the dead (see chaps. 4–5). The Pharisees took the lead in the second wave of persecution. It began with the death of Stephen and was vigorously carried out by Saul of Tarsus. God brought good out of this by scattering believers throughout many areas (see chap. 8; 11:19-26).

The persecution under Herod Agrippa was the first one to be spearheaded by civil authorities. It focused on the apostles. The king apparently believed that if the leaders were killed the movement would die. Whereas the persecution by Saul of Tarsus was motivated by differences in ideologies or religions, the persecution by Herod was politically motivated. He launched his attack on the church **because he saw it pleased the Jews. The Jews** here refers to those Jews who were opposed to Christ and His followers. Herod's practice was to gain political power by pleasing the rich and powerful of the land. Thus his action was done to advance his own ambitions.

Stretched forth his hands refers to Herod's laying his hands on **certain** leaders **of the church** with evil intent. He quickly showed this when **he killed James . . . with the sword.** A sword could be used either to behead a person (the Roman way) or to run a person through with a sword (the Jewish way). We do not know which way was used to kill James. **James** was the apostle James, not the half brother of Jesus mentioned in verse 17. The **James** who was killed was **the brother of John.** James, John, and Peter were the inner circle of the twelve during the life of Jesus. Paul called them the "pillars" of the Jerusalem church (Gal. 2:9). When James and John had come to Jesus asking to sit at His right and left hands, Jesus, referring to His death, asked them if they were able to drink from the cup from which He would drink. When they said they were, Jesus stated they indeed would do so (Mark 10:35-45). We see that prophecy partially fulfilled here. James was the first of the apostles to become a martyr.

When Herod realized this act raised him in the popular esteem, he put **Peter** in **prison.** Herod did not immediately execute him because it was during **the days of unleavened bread.** This seven-day feast followed Passover, which is here translated **Easter.** Herod intended after the feast **to bring him forth to the people** ("to bring him out for public trial," NIV).

Herod was careful to ensure that Peter would not escape or be rescued. He assigned **four quaternions** [kwah-TUHR-nih-uhn] **of soldiers to keep him** ("four squads of four soldiers each to guard him," HCSB).

These verses remind us of several facts about persecution. For one thing, persecution is a special form of discrimination or denial of human rights. To be called *persecution,* it must be directed against Christians precisely because they are followers of Christ. Herod directed his wrath against **the church.** This kind of persecution has taken place down through the centuries. We may think of persecution as having occurred primarily during the early centuries of Christian history, but more people were killed for the cause of Jesus during the 20th century than in all previous centuries combined.[1]

A second fact about persecution is that motivations for persecution vary. Sometimes the reasons are more political than religious. This was the case with Herod, who wanted to please his constituents. The persecution he initiated was not ideological, but it was designed to advance his political career. With Saul of Tarsus the motivation was ideological. Among the worst countries for persecution today are lands under the domination of militant Islam or atheistic Communism.

These persecutions are ideological with political overtones. In a book that ranks countries by the severity of the persecution of Christians, North Korea is among the worst. "Today, virtually all outward vestiges of religion have been wiped out, and North Korea is regarded as the most hard-line atheistic nation in the world."[2]

A third fact is that some persecutions are instigated by the civil authorities and some by individuals or mobs of people. The mob who wanted to kill Paul in Ephesus was made up of people who earned their living making idols. In that situation the civil authorities actually saved Paul (19:22-41). Rome took a tolerant view of Christianity for several decades because they thought it was only a branch of Judaism. During the 60's, Nero was the first emperor to instigate a persecution in Rome. Other later emperors followed his lead.

A fourth fact is that persecution takes many forms—all the way from torture and death to nothing more than ridicule. Some ridicule is about the closest thing to persecution that Americans experience. Christians in lands such as Iran and North Korea know many more violent forms of persecution: "The atrocities include torture, enslavement, rape, imprisonment, forcible separation of children from parents, killings, and massacres—abuses that threaten the very survival of entire Christian communities."[3]

Prayer (Acts 12:5)

Why did the church pray? How did they pray? What lessons does this verse have for us?

Verse 5: **Peter therefore was kept in prison: but prayer was made without ceasing of the church unto God for him.**

While **Peter** awaited his fate **in prison,** believers in the Jerusalem **church** prayed **for him.** Further, **prayer was made without ceasing. Without ceasing** translates *ektenos.* When applied to time, this word means to "continue" or "persevere." When applied to effort, it means to "be earnest" or "fervent." Thus the word in verse 5 can be rendered **without ceasing** ("constant," NKJV), or it can be rendered "earnestly" (NIV, HCSB) or "fervently" (NASB, NRSV). Since both of these are qualities of true prayer, either or both were practiced as the church prayed for Peter. No doubt they were earnest, and very likely they kept on praying.

What can Christians in the United States do to help our persecuted brothers and sisters in other lands? We can pray for them. And we can pray for their persecutors. To do this, we need to be aware of and sensitive to what is happening. The Ethics and Religious Liberty Commission Web site (www.erlc.com) contains links to other organizations working on behalf of the persecuted. Helpful Web sites include www.persecuted-church.org (the official web site for the International Day of Prayer for Persecuted Christians) and www.persecution.com (The Voice of the Martyrs).

The International Mission Board also reports on persecution around the world and requests prayer for those who suffer for their faith. For example, recently they reported the story of a new believer in West Africa who was tortured but refused to deny his Lord and Savior. After his release he said, "While I was being beaten, I thought, they did this to Jesus too. Why should I be different? Our blood is fertilizer for the gospel. When the history of Christianity among our people is told, our names will be remembered among those who were faithful."

In addition to praying, we can seek to influence our government to use its influence to help persecuted people. Too often, political and economic concerns take precedence over human rights, especially religious freedom. We need to appreciate true religious freedom as one of our greatest blessings. This is the freedom on which all the others rest. It is no accident that the first part of the First Amendment of our Constitution, which was Article I of The Bill of Rights, guarantees freedom of religion.

The closest we in America get to persecution is facing ridicule from non-Christians. As we pray for courage for people facing death, we also need to pray for boldness to live for Christ in spite of ridicule.

Power (Acts 12:6-10)

How could Peter sleep under such circumstances? How did the Lord deliver him? Why does God deliver some but not others?

Verses 6-10: And when Herod would have brought him forth, the same night Peter was sleeping between two soldiers, bound with two chains: and the keepers before the door kept the prison. ⁷And, behold, the angel of the Lord came upon him, and a light shined in the prison: and he smote Peter on the side, and raised him up, saying, Arise up quickly. And his chains fell off from his hands. ⁸And the angel said unto him, Gird thyself, and bind on thy sandals. And so he did. And he saith unto him, Cast thy garment about thee, and follow me. ⁹And he went out, and followed him; and wist not that it was true which was done by the angel; but thought he saw

a vision. **¹⁰When they were past the first and the second ward, they came unto the iron gate that leadeth unto the city; which opened to them of his own accord: and they went out, and passed on through one street; and forthwith the angel departed from him.**

In the phrase **when Herod would have brought him forth,** the Greek word *proagagein* means to "lead forth" or "bring forth." The *New International Version* adds "to trial"; the *Holman Christian Standard Bible* adds "for execution." Since there is no record of a trial for James before he was executed, we may surmise that Herod was going to bring Peter out for execution. At least this seems to have been the expectation of those gathered in Mary's home (see their statement in v. 15b).

The description of Peter's deliverance reads as if the action were in slow motion, so that each detail would be clear. Verse 6 describes how securely Peter was being guarded. He was probably in the Tower of Antonia, at one corner of the temple complex. This is where the Roman troops were barracked. Roman night duty was divided into four shifts of three hours each. Peter was chained to two soldiers with two others as sentries.

The angel of the Lord was sent to deliver Peter. The apostle was sleeping soundly, no doubt entrusting himself into the hands of the Lord. The angel **smote** ("poked," CEV) **Peter on the side. Smote** is the same word used later in the chapter of the angel smiting Herod Agrippa I and bringing about his death (v. 23). The word means to strike a blow, usually with force. One was a saving touch; the other was a touch of judgment.

This was not Peter's *escape,* it was his *deliverance.* As they **went out,** we see the power of the Lord demonstrated dramatically. First, Peter's **chains fell off from his hands.** Then Peter and the angel passed through **the first and the second ward.** Finally **they came unto the iron gate that leadeth unto the city,** and—wonder of wonders—it **opened to them of** its **own accord.** From there **they went out, and passed on through one street** together before **the angel departed from** Peter. All of this happened without the soldiers to whom Peter was chained, or any of the soldiers in the facility, hearing them and waking up!

Why was Peter spared and James killed? We don't know the answer, except to say that it was not God's time for Peter. Tradition records that Peter later did give his life, but the Lord had much for him to do before his death. Sometimes the Lord answers our prayers by delivering us *from* a threatening situation; at other times He delivers us *through* it; still at other times He allows us to die. God always has the *power*, but deliverance may not always be His *purpose*. Whatever the individual situation may be, dying as a faithful Christian means immediate entrance into the presence of the Lord.

Proof (Acts 12:11-17)

When did Peter realize that he had been delivered? Where did he decide to go? What kind of reception did he receive? Why did the believers think Rhoda was crazy? What does their reaction teach about their prayers? How does verse 17 show that the Lord's work goes on?

Verses 11-16: And when Peter was come to himself, he said, Now I know of a surety, that the Lord hath sent his angel, and hath delivered me out of the hand of Herod, and from all the expectation of the people of the Jews. ¹²And when he had considered the thing, he came to the house of Mary the mother of John, whose surname was Mark; where many were gathered together praying. ¹³And as Peter knocked at the door of the gate, a damsel came to hearken, named Rhoda. ¹⁴And when she knew Peter's voice, she opened not the gate for gladness, but ran in, and told how Peter stood before the gate. ¹⁵And they said unto her, Thou art mad. But she constantly affirmed that it was even so. Then said they, It is his angel. ¹⁶But Peter continued knocking: and when they had opened the door, and saw him, they were astonished.

During the time of being delivered step by step, Peter thought he was seeing **a vision** or having a dream. However, when the angel departed leaving him safely outside the prison, Peter came **to himself.** He then realized that **the Lord** used **his angel** to save him from the clutches of the evil king.

Peter headed for **the house of Mary.** This **Mary** is not one of the three mentioned in the Gospels. She was a well-to-do believer who opened her house for the church in Jerusalem to use as a meeting place. Her son was **John, whose surname was Mark.** He is mentioned because of his later prominence.

The house had a courtyard, and **Peter knocked at the door of the gate.** The person responsible for the gate was a young woman named **Rhoda.** When she went to the door, she recognized **Peter's voice.** However, rather than opening the gate, she was so excited that she ran in and told the others that Peter was outside. They said, **Thou art mad** ("crazy," CEV, REB, HCSB; "out of your mind," NASB, NIV, NRSV; "beside yourself,"

NKJV). The same word appears in 26:24, where Festus told Paul he was insane. The word is *maine,* from which we get our word *maniac.*

When Rhoda stuck to her story they said, **It is his angel.** Many people believe in a guardian angel for each person. This belief is based on this verse and Matthew 18:10. The New Testament evidence for angels watching over us is stronger than the case for one angel assigned for life to each person. John B. Polhill suggested a different meaning: "This response reflects the Jewish belief that each person has a guardian angel as his or her spiritual counterpart. It was believed that one's angel often appeared immediately after the person's death, and that idea may lurk behind the response to Rhoda. 'You've seen his ghost,' we would say."[4]

Peter continued knocking. Finally they opened the gate and saw that it was Peter—and **they were astonished.** What does this say about their confidence in having their prayers answered? They had been earnestly and persistently praying to God for Peter's deliverance. When he came to the door, they could not believe it was he. And when they saw him, they were astonished. This shows they had little faith that God would actually answer their prayer. How many of our prayers are like theirs? We ask for something, but we don't really expect God to do it.

***Verse 17:* But he, beckoning unto them with the hand to hold their peace, declared unto them how the Lord had brought him out of the prison. And he said, Go show these things unto James, and to the brethren. And he departed, and went into another place.**

Peter wasted no time getting down to business. He had been delivered once; he did not want to presume that the Lord would do it again. He realized that it was time for him to move on. The Lord had used him mightily in Jerusalem, but he was not the only leader available. Thus he told the church to "tell" (NKJV, NIV, NRSV) or "report" (NASB, HCSB) **these things unto James, and to the brethren.** This **James** was the half brother of Jesus. During Jesus' ministry His brothers did not believe (John 7:5), but Jesus appeared to James after His resurrection (1 Cor. 15:7) and James was with the believers before Pentecost (Acts 1:14). He also wrote the Letter of James. After Peter left, James became the leader of the Jerusalem church. He continued in this role even when Peter later was able to return to Jerusalem after the death of Herod Agrippa I (15:7,13). According to Josephus, James, like Peter, later gave his life for Christ. But for many years he provided leadership for the Jerusalem church.

Peter **departed, and went into another place.** Some Christian groups insist that he went to Rome. This is unlikely since Paul's later letter to Rome says nothing about this. The tradition is strong that Peter eventually went to Rome, but not at this time.

One lasting lesson of this verse is that leaders come and go, but the Lord continues His work using other leaders. No leader is indispensable to the Lord's work. This is the Lord's work, and He will cause His kingdom to come and His will to be done.

❖ Spiritual Transformations

Herod Agrippa I executed James the apostle and put Peter in prison when he saw that this pleased the people. The church prayed earnestly and persistently for Peter. God sent an angel, who delivered Peter from a secure prison. When Peter showed up where the church was praying, they at first refused to believe it was Peter. The apostle turned the work in Jerusalem over to James the half brother of Jesus, and Peter went to serve in other places.

One impact this lesson should have on our lives is to help us be advocates on behalf of fellow believers who are being persecuted. Summing up the applications of this lesson: Many Christians are being persecuted, especially in lands controlled by militant Islam or atheistic Communism. The persecution takes the form of everything from ridicule to death. Some persecutions are sponsored by governments; some are carried out by mobs. American Christians can pray for persecuted believers and influence our government to bring pressure to bear on the worst offenders. In addition, we can thank God for the freedom we have. We also can resolve not to let the threat of ridicule silence our own witness for the Lord.

What can you do to help those who are persecuted? _____
What will you commit to do? _____

Prayer of Commitment: Lord, be with those who are persecuted for Your name's sake. Give them courage to be faithful to You. Amen.

[1]Nina Shea, *In the Lion's Den* [Nashville: Broadman & Holman Publishers, 1997], 1.
[2]Paul Marshall, ed., *Religious Freedom in the World* [Nashville: Broadman & Holman Publishers, 2000], 189.
[3]Shea, *In the Lion's Den*, 2.
[4]Polhill, "Acts," NAC, 282.